What on Earth
Are You Doing?

Jesus' Call to World Mission

What on Earth Are You Doing?

Michael Griffiths

BAKER BOOK HOUSE

Grand Rapids, Michigan 49506

Reprinted 1983 by
Baker Book House
with permission of copyright owner
and Inter-Varsity Press, England

ISBN: 0-8010-3792-1

Printed in the United States of America

Quotations from the Bible are from the
New International Version, © 1978 by the
New York International Bible Society,
published in Great Britain by
Hodder and Stoughton Ltd.

Typeset in 10/11 Baskerville
by Nuprint Services Ltd, Harpenden, Herts.

Contents

Preface

This is a straightforward book about contemporary missionary work. It is intended to motivate, inform, reassure and challenge Christians. There is a continuing need for substantial numbers of them to leave countries where the number of churches and believers is relatively high, to help to build new congregations where Christians are few and thinly spread.

The contents (apart from the final chapter) were presented more or less in this form as the annual Baker Book Lecture, given at the Reformed Bible College, Grand Rapids, Michigan in February 1982. A part of chapter four was originally given as an address at 'Mission '80', organized by the European Missionary Association in Lausanne, Switzerland after Christmas, 1979.

I would like to thank both the Publishers and my kind friend Dick van Halsema, President of the Reformed Bible College, for their encouragement in commissioning and delivery of this material, and in its preparation for publication. I would also like to thank Doreen Bairstow for typing the manuscript, and the London Bible College for releasing me during term-time to give the lectures.

Thanks are also due to the Overseas Missionary Fellowship (formerly the China Inland Mission) in whose ranks my wife and I were privileged to serve for twenty-three years. Though many other things have changed during those years, the population of many countries has doubled for example, it is striking that the need for (the right kind of) missionaries has in no way diminished, and perhaps even increased.

I am also grateful for the way that the Baker Book House in Grand Rapids has been prepared to pass over editorial responsibilities to the Inter-Varsity Press in Britain, with whom I have a much-appreciated relationship that began with a booklet in my own student days. This kind of sensible co-operation between Christian organizations ought to be more common than it is. But the aim of all this activity by many people has been to get the book into your hands so that you can do something about it – so please read on!

Michael Griffiths
April, 1983

One
What kind of God is he?

Objectives:
To show that God reveals himself in the Bible to be an outgoing 'missionary' God in his communication with us; supremely in Jesus Christ who goes to all sorts of people; and continuing till today in the outgoing work of the Holy Spirit. Because he is a missionary God so we should be missionary people.

We begin with God. What kind of a God is he? The God of the Bible may be described as the Outgoing God. He is not isolated, distant, withdrawn or remote – but a welcoming, close at hand, involved, warm, loving Person.

In our childhood days, and throughout life, from time to time we meet individual adults to whom we are drawn by the warmth and attractiveness of their personalities. As children we wanted to draw close, sit on their knees, get them to tell us stories: as adults we want to enjoy their company, listen to what they have to say, try to spark off ideas and see what we can learn from them. The *Readers Digest* feature 'The Most Unforgettable Character' speaks of these sort of people. The God of the Bible is like all of these 'unforgettable' and attractive personalities rolled into one – only superlatively more so. Tozer described God as being 'the most winsome of all Beings'.

This *outgoingness* of God allows us to call him 'the mission-

9

ary God'. Peter quotes the repeated theme of Leviticus, 'Be holy, because I am holy' (1 Peter 1:15), while Paul tells us to imitate God, as dearly loved children, to lead a life of love, just as Christ loved us . . . (Ephesians 5:1–2). And the great motivation for our missionary outreach is as simple as that. Because God is an outgoing missionary God, you who call yourselves his children must be like him in this as well. What the Bible is saying is 'Be missionary because I am a missionary . . .' or in a more obvious direct quotation, 'As the Father has sent me, I am sending you' (John 20:21).

Stephen, that original thinker

Have you ever wondered why Luke, with only one long roll of papyrus to write Acts, devoted quite so much space to Stephen? Why on earth include fifty-two verses* of Stephen's speech? Stephen had been accused of saying that Jesus would change the Jewish Law and destroy the Jewish temple in Jerusalem. His defence reveals him to be the outstanding thinker and theologian of the early church. The Jews saw Israel and the temple in Jerusalem as the central focus of everything. Stephen points out that God revealed himself to their forefather Abraham in Mesopotamia and not in Israel. That God was with Joseph in Egypt. He even reminds them, somewhat mischievously, that Joseph and his father Jacob (Israel himself) were not buried in Jerusalem, but in Samaria among the despised Samaritans. Every Jew knew that Moses died without entering the promised land at all, but Stephen points out that the holy ground where the Lord gave the Law to Moses was in Arab territory.

Stephen was saying that God is not limited to Israel or to the Jerusalem temple: he is the outgoing God, who revealed himself to the Jewish patriarchs before they had entered the promised land at all. The Pentateuch, the five books of

* *Cf.* Paul on Mars' Hill 10 verses; Peter at Pentecost 22 verses; Paul before Agrippa 26 verses.

Moses, are nearly all about what happened outside of Israel. No wonder the Jewish leaders gnashed their ethnocentric teeth at him. God is not limited by geography: he is the outgoing, missionary God who goes out to look for people, and speaks to them wherever he wishes.

God is a missionary God

On average God is mentioned as doing something in every other verse of Stephen's speech. It is *God* who speaks to Abraham in Mesopotamia; it is *God* who is with Joseph in Egypt; it is *God* who reveals himself to Moses at Sinai. God is always moving out. He is not a stationary God, who works only within a circumscribed area. The goddess Diana of the Ephesians fell down from heaven (Acts 19:35) being apparently incapable of independent movement. The God of the Bible is not like that. He is a God who goes out to people wherever they are and whoever they are, so that 'Everyone who calls on the name of the Lord will be saved' (Romans 10:13).

Once you have seen this, it stares at you throughout the Old Testament. He is the seeking God, the Shepherd of his people, ever concerned to bring Israel back to himself each time they go astray. The Bible is not the record of sheep looking for the lost shepherd, but of the Shepherd God seeking for his foolish stubborn straying people, and bringing them back again and again.

Right at the beginning we read of Adam and Eve disobedient and hiding away – and the Lord God looking for them and calling 'Where are you?' (Genesis 3:9).

It is God who reveals himself to Abraham in Mesopotamia and promises that through him 'all peoples on earth' will be blessed (Genesis 12:3), the charter of Gentile evangelism.

It is God who sent Joseph to Egypt, as Joseph is at pains to point out to his embarrassed and terrified brothers: 'God sent me ahead of you' (Genesis 45:5–8).

11

It is God who sends Moses to bring Israel out of Egypt and into the promised land. The Lord says, '*I* have indeed seen the misery of my people. . . . *I* have heard them crying. . . . *I* am concerned about their suffering. So *I* have come down to rescue them. . . . So now, go. *I* am *sending you.* . . .' (Exodus 3:7–10). It is Moses who is reluctant to leave the peaceful pastoral scene and the comfortable life with Zipporah his wife and baby Gershom, and who spends two chapters of Exodus trying to persuade the Lord that he is insufficiently qualified to go. It is God who wants action and outgoing.

It is God who, through Jeremiah the prophet, tells Israel: 'From the time your forefathers left Egypt until now, *day after day, again and again I sent you my servants* the prophets . . .' (Jeremiah 7:25).

It is God who sends Jonah (another reluctant envoy) to Nineveh, as well as sending messages to many other Gentile nations through the prophets. Although the prophets are Jews and their ministry is chiefly to Judah and Israel, they nearly always have things to say to the nations on their borders as well.

In the Psalms there are seventy-six references to the 'nations', even though the Psalms are part of the worship of Israel. And if you add references to 'all the earth' and 'the peoples' it is quite startling to see how much the Psalms teach us of God's concern for all mankind.

There is no need to labour this, but a quotation from the prophets about the Lord's attitude to Israel shows the kind of Person that God is: 'I revealed myself to those who did not ask for me; I was found by those who did not seek me. To a nation that did not call on my name, I said: 'Here am I, here am I'. All day long I have held out my hands to an obstinate people . . .' (Isaiah 65:1–2). He is a Person who reaches out to people.

Now this should speak to us. We should be excited about it.

God's people are outgoing people

The characters that the Outgoing God chooses and calls have to become outgoing people.

Abraham is commanded, 'Leave your country, your people and your father's household and go to the land I will show you . . .' (Genesis 12:1). And so Abraham obeys God and goes out, not knowing where he is going. 'By faith he made his home in the promised land, like a stranger in a foreign country' (Hebrews 11:9). He left behind the civilization of Ur to go far from home to a new place, an adventure of faith. God's call is to go out to new adventure.

Joseph had no choice: circumstances had already been overruled to bring him into Egypt as a slave sold off by his brothers. This rather spoiled child, with his long-sleeved coat of many colours, boasting tactlessly about his dreams, now becomes a man – rising to responsibility first in the house of Potiphar, then in the prison and finally in the court of Pharaoh. He even became known among the surrounding nations. He gives an extraordinary display of courage, persistence and administrative ability. Though he is an alien, he rises to the top – and all because the Outgoing God is 'with him'. As a cross-cultural 'missionary' he is quite remarkable, as an outgoing man.

Moses when he grew up refused to be called the son of Pharaoh's daughter (Hebrews 11:24ff.). He was ready to leave his education and the treasures of Egypt in order to identify with a slave rabble and lead them out into the wilderness, in spite of their rebellious ingratitude. Moses is an outstanding example of the life of faith, risking his life in order to save not only his own but the lives of many others.

He who would save his life will lose it. He who is ready to lose it, will find it. That such choices were not easily made is quite clear. But this is what the Outgoing God does for those who trust him: he leads them out into all kinds of new and exciting ventures, using them to bless others, and blessing them through it all. But it is an adventure *with*

13

God, who promises to be with them (Exodus 3:12; James 2:23), and us.

To respond to the missionary God is not a restricting call to a dull limited life, but a call to adventure, to agony and ecstasy, to lead a far fuller and more fulfilling life than we could ever have devised for ourselves. God is the Outgoing God, and those who respond to his call become adventurous people of faith, like Abraham, Joseph and Moses.

The outgoing power of the Spirit

Though the Old Testament has a place for the nations, the Jews of the first century nonetheless had a Jerusalem-centred, temple-focused view of the world. Jerusalem was the navel of the earth. They were just as ethnocentric as most nations are still to this day. Look at a school atlas in the United States, or Britain, or Japan, and you will see what I mean. Each country shows the projection of the world with itself in the centre – and the continental land masses have to be rearranged accordingly, even if you have to separate Europe from Asia to do it! China indeed calls itself the Middle Kingdom, but everyone else thinks that way about their own country too. The Jews then saw the possibility of salvation for the nations – if they came up to Jerusalem to worship, as the Ethiopian official did (Acts 8:27). They must become proselytes accepting the sign of circumcision, Jewish food laws and culture. Many of the early Christians took a long time to get away from this view, and even today there are still some Christians who seem to have a Jerusalem focus to their thinking.

The Jews had a centripetal view of the world with Jerusalem at its centre and all the nations coming to the old Jerusalem to worship.

The message of Acts is to throw that whole view into reverse. 'You will receive power when the Holy Spirit comes on you; and you will be my witnesses in Jerusalem, and in all Judea and Samaria, and to the ends of the earth,' promised

14

Jesus before his ascension (Acts 1:8). His words not only outline the progress of the early church as it spread in outgoing ripples from Jerusalem, but also provide a useful outline for the book of Acts. It tells us that the power of the Spirit of the Outgoing God is a centrifugal force that flings them out towards the frontiers. No longer do the Gentiles have to come in as the Jews expected them to do. Now the witnesses have to go out – to the ends of the earth.

In the early chapters however the apostles do not yet seem to have grasped this. They begin by asking the resurrected Christ whether he will at this time 'restore the kingdom to Israel' (1:6), and they are temple-centred, observing the hour of prayer (3:1), preaching and teaching boldly in the temple courts in the power of the Spirit (5:12). Some of them were still thinking in these terms when Paul returned from his third missionary journey having planted churches all over present day Turkey and Greece. They wanted him to go up to the temple and to take vows there (21:23ff.).

We have already questioned Luke's purpose in giving so much prominence to Stephen's speech, and to the appointment of the Seven to serve tables and care for the widows. Why on earth *was* this so significant?

Because these events introduce us to the Hellenistic Jews. The seven men chosen all have Greek names and indeed one of them had been born a Gentile, Nicolas the proselyte from Antioch. Great stress is laid on their spirituality. 'Choose seven men . . . known to be *full of the Spirit* and wisdom . . . they chose Stephen, a man *full of* faith and of *the Holy Spirit* . . . a man *full of God's grace* and power' (Acts 6:3–8). Stephen then engages in argument with Hellenistic Jews: (verses 9ff.) Jews of Cyrene in North Africa, where Lucius one of the original Antioch Christians came from; Jews of Alexandria, like the eloquent Apollos who went on from Ephesus to Corinth; Jews of Cilicia who must surely have included among them a Jew from its chief city, Tarsus, called Saul.

These Hellenistic Jews were people of much wider and more liberal outlook than Jews who had never been outside Palestine. They were people with their minds enlarged by contact with two cultures and their literature – both the Hebrew and the Greek: much as today overseas Chinese have a much wider outlook than those who have never been out of mainland China. They had grown up in the Jewish communities of the Dispersion, born overseas from Israel, but contact with other countries and travel had broadened their education. They took great pride in their Jewish roots, however, and that is why they were so angry with Stephen when he questioned their Jerusalem-centredness. The Hellenistic Jews were a natural bridge group whom God used to reach out to the nations. The people, gathered in Jerusalem on the day of Pentecost, were Hellenistic Jews (Acts 2:9–11). The men full of wisdom, faith and the Holy Spirit, whom the Outgoing Spirit used to spread the gospel, were Hellenistic Jews. They saw that the gospel could not be contained merely in a sect of Judaism, and that it was of supranational and universal importance.

Stephen was among the first to think like this; a far-sighted spokesman. As Abraham, Joseph and Moses had gone out, so must they. And all the early pioneers of outreach seem to have belonged to this group. Stephen and Philip were Hellenists; so were Barnabas of Cyprus and Saul of Tarsus: and the men of Cyprus and Cyrene who pioneered the new mixed Gentile and Jewish congregation at Antioch.

Stephen's thought seems to have influenced Saul's. This new way of looking at Scripture was germinal in developing the theology of the apostle to the Gentiles. When Saul was converted it was Stephen's approach to the Old Testament that he followed as he rethought his whole theology with Jesus the Messiah at its centre. When he went back to Jerusalem for the first time he also debated with the Hellenistic Jews (Acts 9:29).

Outgoing, Spirit-filled people

It was Stephen's speech and consequent martyrdom which occasioned and stimulated the break-out from a Jerusalem-imprisoned Christianity, first to Samaria and then to the ends of the earth.

Chapter 8 tells us that a persecution broke out because of Stephen and that all the Christians except the apostles were scattered throughout Judea and Samaria (a significant allusion back to Acts 1:8), that Philip went and preached to the Samaritans, and that the Outgoing Holy Spirit showed that even the mixed-race Samaritans could be Christians.

It was the Holy Spirit, we are told, who instructed Philip to hitch a lift with the Ethiopian official (8:29) and so the Outgoing Spirit brings the first African convert to baptism through Philip's ministry.

Chapter 9 tells us of the conversion and baptism of Saul of Tarsus – ironically not in Jerusalem, but at Damascus in Syria.

Chapters 10 and 11 tell us about the significant precedent set by Peter under the prompting of the Holy Spirit. Peter was learning, but slowly. At Joppa he was staying with Simon the tanner: in itself a mark of grace, for tanners were a despised social group discriminated against by the Jews. Tanners were not permitted to practise their trade in Jerusalem, and a woman could get a divorce from a tanner if she couldn't stand the smell. It was the Outgoing God who gave Peter his vision of the unclean animals – and we are told specifically that it was the Holy Spirit who told him not to hesitate about going with the three messengers who had come from the Gentile centurion, Cornelius. So he travelled up the coast to Caesarea where the Holy Spirit came on the Gentiles. Peter had to explain his actions to his Jewish brethren. Why had he gone into the house of uncircumcised men and eaten with them? He explained the vision, and twice mentioned the guidance of the Spirit: and thus they concluded, and it's difficult to avoid the impression that the

17

words were grudging or incredulous, 'So then, God has even granted to the Gentiles repentance unto life' (11:18). From this time onwards the Spirit-led outreach to the Gentiles gains increasing momentum.

In chapter 13 the Outgoing Spirit tells the Antioch church to set aside Barnabas and Saul for the work to which he has called them, and the first church-planting expeditions to Asia Minor, and then to Greece and Europe are launched.

In all this we can see the Outgoing Spirit leading and prompting his servants to reach out, often against their cultural preconceptions and in spite of their racial prejudice. This is what God is like: he pushes people to go out.

The Outgoing Christ

This same pattern of *outgoingness* is nowhere more evident than in the ministry of Jesus. The Light of the World, the Good Shepherd, the True and Living Way – all these titles remind us that he came to seek and save that which was lost. But it is the actions of Jesus that demonstrate most clearly what kind of Person God is: the most winsome Outgoing One.

He is for ever going out, being criticized for it, breaking through the barriers of human reserve, prejudice or sense of what is proper. He is accused of being the friend of publicans and sinners when he participates in banquets in the homes of tax-collectors Matthew (Levi) and Zacchaeus. He speaks to a sinful Samaritan woman, so that his disciples are astonished. He takes children into his arms when the disciples think he is too busy. He touches the leper whom everyone else would shrink from touching. He refuses to be bound by human social barriers – and makes despised Samaritans, shepherds and tax-collectors the heroes of his parables. He has time for Samaritans and for Gentiles such as the centurion and Syrophoenician woman. He sets us a clear pattern for inner-city work, for seeking to heal the wounds of racial and social groups regarded as second-class citizens in our societies. He will talk to anyone, and all sorts of people want to talk to him.

The very fact of his coming at all demonstrates his outgoingness. He humbled and emptied himself (Philippians 2:7–8). Though he was rich, for our sakes he became poor (2 Corinthians 8:9). His incarnation shows the lengths to which he was prepared to go. He is not ashamed to call us brothers. He shared our humanity, our flesh and blood. He knows our feelings, understands our weaknesses (Hebrews 2:11, 14, 17; 4:15). What greater act of missionary identification could there be: the eternal Son of God came down to earth from heaven and was born as a human baby. He had to be carried about totally dependent on humans to clothe, feed, nurse and wash him. The words of the hymn, 'Lo, he abhors not the virgin's womb' express this real missionary identification.

To become a missionary you must be born again once more. You become a cultural baby. You make noises, but nobody knows what you are trying to say: the speech of others around you is incomprehensible; you are reduced like a baby to inane smiling as the only possible form of communication. The adult human has to humble himself to become incarnate in a new society. But it is very partial identification compared with his, who set us a missionary pattern: 'As the Father has sent me, I am sending you . . .' (John 20:21).

The supreme demonstration of God's missionary character is shown in the death of Jesus on our behalf. His love leads him to extreme lengths, 'even death on a cross'. He is ready to be humiliated, publicly scoffed at, stripped of clothes, torn from friends and family – all to save us. He is a Saviour who goes to passionate extremes. This is the value he sets on human beings – they are so precious to him that he will give up all for them. 'I am sending you' means that we too must be ready to sacrifice everything in order to save human beings. Africans, Indians and Chinese will be so dear to us that we also will go to extreme lengths to give ourselves

19

for them, to sacrifice our lives to win them to Jesus Christ. He loved us enough to wash our filthy feet, and make them beautiful on the mountains as bearers of good news. 'I am sending you' means that we love people enough to empty and humble ourselves to take the good news to them.

This is the kind of God, the kind of Person he is. And he now wants us to be the kind of person who loves and cares and will go to drastic lengths to show it. He is a Good Friday God; we are to be Man Friday for him.

Conclusion

If this is what God is like – if he is thus the Outgoing One, then there is a challenge to us, to break the fetters of our reserve and clannishness. We too can be very centripetal in our approach. We talk of 'outreach' when we mean 'in-drag'. We think principally of getting people into a church building where they can be preached at by a religious professional, whereas the Spirit wants to thrust us out with centrifugal force to go where needy men and women are, to reach them with the gospel. We are not to stay in our social, ethnic and religious ghettos, but to venture boldly in the power of the Spirit to stay with tanners, hitch-hike with Ethiopians, dance for joy with beggars, feast with tax-collectors, embrace Samaritans as brothers and to be liberated from the fetters of our social and ethnic reserve by the missionary Christ. The automobile is a terrible device for shutting us away from other people and the high-rise apartment block is almost worse. Human self-centredness, even in Christians, means that we are so busy going where we want to go, and doing what we want to do, that we can live largely ignorant of the needs of those around us. This denies the kind of God to whom we belong, the Saviour who died for us and the Spirit who indwells us.

If Jesus were here what would he do? To whom would he speak? Jesus did not communicate merely with his own peer group. Old men and old women, young men and young women, children – none were beneath his dignity, outside his concern and interest.

The Outgoing God, then, calls us to wildness and risk and humility and love. We have quite deliberately started with God. If you start with man you start worrying about your future, your profession, your bank balance, your children and a hundred and one reasons for doing nothing. But if you start with theology – and with God, then it all looks quite different. The perspective is right. If he cares for mankind and puts such a value on them, and if he loves me like this, then I must go out and love them too. Look at God first, then you can see human beings properly, with new eyes. That simple Indian peasant or that sophisticated Japanese businessman looks different in the light of the cross.

Check: Does this characteristic of God as outgoing motivate you to be more outgoing in your attitude to others, especially those of different racial groups? If not, start again, and think some more!

Two
Are people all right as they are?

Objectives:
To make us aware of the spiritual need of people apart from Christ and who have never heard the gospel by expounding Ephesians 2:1–4, 11–13.

We have started with God. Now we go on to think about man in his need. Many of us today are so wrapped up in the cosy cocoon of our humanism that it is difficult for us to grasp the reality of human need in countries where most people are without Christ. The two-thirds world seems so far away from the materialistic West. We read of the horrors of war, terror and starvation in Kampuchea or famine in Bangladesh or Northern Kenya, and if we have imagination, we shudder and thank God that we don't have to live there. Perhaps we even give something to help, but we soon forget, and all that is happening out there seems so remote from our own materialistic consumer society.

An earlier generation was deeply moved by the writing of Amy Carmichael of Dohnavur about the need of Hindu India where small children were sold to the temple for prostitution. There are still countries like Thailand and Japan where a bad harvest may mean a similar fate for impoverished farmers' daughters, but by and large social conditions have improved to such an extent in Western countries that the horrors of the nineteenth century seem far away. Even so, Amy Carmichael used one very famous illustration which I think still makes a deep impression:

> The tom-toms thumped straight on all night, and the darkness shuddered round me like a living, feeling thing. I could not go to sleep, so I lay awake and looked; and I saw, as it seemed, this: That I stood on a grassy sward, and at my feet a precipice broke sheer down into infinite space. I looked, but saw no bottom; only cloud shapes, black and furiously coiled, and great shadow-shrouded hollows, and unfathomable depths. Back I drew, dizzy at the depth. Then I saw forms of people moving single file along the grass. They were making for the edge. There was a woman with a baby in her arms and another little child holding on to her dress. She was on the very verge. Then I saw that she was blind. She lifted her foot for the next step . . . it trod air. She was over, and the children with her. Oh, the cry as they went over.
>
> And over these gaps the people fell in their blindness, quite unwarned; and the green grass seemed blood-red to me, and the gulf yawned like the mouth of hell. Then I saw, like a picture of peace, a group of people under some trees, with their backs turned towards the gulf. They were making daisy chains. Sometimes when a piercing shriek cut the quiet air and reached them it disturbed them, and they thought it rather a vulgar noise. And if one of their number started up and wanted to go and do something to help, then all the others would pull that one down. 'Why should you get so excited about it? You must wait for a definite call to go! You haven't finished your daisy chains yet.'
>
> *Things As They Are*

Christians face criticism from those who question the need or even the ethics of seeking to bring people to Christ. 'You Christians are so intolerant,' they say: 'these people are

23

quite all right as they are, sincere in their religious beliefs, so why interfere with their religion and their culture?'

Others would say, 'Surely those old Victorian ideas about millions in heathen darkness perishing and bowing down to idols of wood and stone were a form of racial superiority that we now recognize to be wrong.' Yes, perhaps there was something of that smug superiority then, and vestiges of it left today also. We recognize that people can be just as lost and perishing in our own society, bowing down to idols of steel and chrome, as any heathen people elsewhere.

How, then, do we respond to these criticisms?

This chapter is based upon Ephesians chapter 2. What does God say about the state of those apart from Christ? The passage is all the more interesting because Paul's intention is to describe the wonders of what Christ has done. 'God made us alive,' he says (verses 4–5). Only incidentally does he speak of sin, because he first has to explain our need to be made alive. Similarly, later, when he is explaining the corporate blessing of belonging to God's household, and being fellow-citizens with God's people, he must first explain the corporate aspects of the sinful world.

Phrases from this passage, such as 'the ways of this world' and 'the ruler of the kingdom of the air', familiar though they may be to church people, just do not seem to relate at first to the everyday twentieth-century situation. Our purpose is to show that this description is indeed extremely relevant today, and this will open our eyes to the miserable state mankind is in.

1. *Programmed and conditioned by culture and society*
This might be an up-to-date translation of *'following the ways of this world'* (verse 2). People's attitudes and religions are largely determined by the country and culture in which they have grown up. Television propaganda and media advertising try to manipulate us to buy the things they want to sell us, and to accept attitudes which they want to condition in us.

24

Japan is a very sophisticated country – full of gadgets from electrically heated toilet seats to closed-circuit television in buses, and totally mechanized ticket checking systems at subway stations. It is also an intensely conformist society. Small children are taught that they will be laughed at if they do not conform. Disobedient children will be locked out of the home and left outside to scream, to be readmitted only when they promise to conform in the future. It is small wonder then that people programmed by society to be submissive robot-like workers for the business companies find it difficult not to conform to normal religious practice as well. It takes independence and courage to join the tiny one-per-cent Christian minority.

If you leave the roads of Peninsular Malaysia, with their small towns made up of the shops of Chinese and Indian merchants, and take to the rivers, you will find a new world of warm, charming and delightful people – the Malays. As a Christian you long to tell them about the Lord Jesus, who loves them and died and rose for them. But if you, a foreigner, did so, you would be ushered out of the country very quickly. The Declaration of Human Rights of the United Nations has this to say about religion:

Everyone has the right to freedom of thought, conscience and religion; this right includes freedom to change his religion or belief, and freedom, either alone or in community with others and in public or private, to manifest his religion or belief in teaching, practice, worship or observance. (Article 18, proclaimed by the United Nations on 10 December 1948.)

But Malaysia, like most other Muslim countries, has never ratified the Declaration of Human Rights. It is not a free country in this regard. In theory a Malay who wishes to enter a church and listen to the gospel may do so, but anyone who encourages him to become a Christian faces trouble.

In fact, very strong social pressure is exerted against people wishing to convert out of Islam. At the same time it is not unknown for inducements to be offered to people if they convert to Islam. People are not really free agents, but the direction of their lives is controlled by 'the ways of this world'. According to the *Shariah* of Islam it is no sin to kill an apostate person, so that it is perilous for a Muslim to try to change his religion. A young Muslim couple in Egypt (a country with a large Christian minority) who decided to become Christians had to disappear, leaving their home and possessions behind in the Muslim quarter, because any indication of their moving out could have been to invite death.

In Nepal anyone being baptized has to face a prison sentence of up to a year, and anyone baptizing others a sentence of up to six years. It is possible to become a Christian and an increasing number of Nepalis are doing so, but the pressure of their Hindu society makes it extremely difficult. Similarly in many Communist countries, while there are Christians, any member of the Communist Party wishing to be a Christian faces sanctions.

2. *Living in fear of hostile spiritual forces*
Even in developed countries there remains a continuing fear of occult evil forces. It is sometimes forgotten that a world without knowledge of the true and living God is not a religionless world, but one in which people live in fear of hostile evil spirits. Both the inhabitants of the ancient world and of tribal communities today see the world as full of malign evil spirits. The air is full of them, so that 'the ruler of the kingdom of the air' is a present reality and not an outmoded superstition as far as most are concerned. Animistic beliefs and fears are much more widespread than is often realized. Frequently a population nominally Buddhist like the Thai, or Islamic in Arab countries, or the Hindus of Bali or village India, have successfully merged the new religion with their basic animistic beliefs. They

26

continue to offer sacrifices and live in superstitious fear of the old gods and spirits of the land.

Even in a sophisticated country like Japan their funeral practices show how much they are still motivated by fear of spirits. The Buddhist's scriptures are meant to help the living to enlightenment and the Buddhist priest is in search of enlightenment. However at the Japanese funeral, the living pay the priests to recite the scriptures to the spirits of the dead! Thus although it is called a 'Buddhist' funeral, the Buddhist scriptures are actually being used as a charm to keep the ghosts of the dead from troubling the living.

In Thailand the so-called 'spirit-houses' outside Thai homes remind us that, in spite of the way in which the whole culture is inextricably enmeshed with Buddhism, the old animistic beliefs die hard. When a Thai person dies, though he has been loved by his family, now suddenly at the moment of death he becomes a hostile evil spirit.

In more primitive tribal communities the demon strings tied on the wrists at birth, the banging of drums and gongs at night to keep the evil spirits away – the world is thronged with hostile evil spirits wreaking their malice upon men.

It is this fear of the spirits which lies behind taboos. The Tagal tribe in Sabah (formerly British North Borneo) had a taboo against women who were pregnant or lactating eating any green vegetables. They were not allowed to eat greens for fear of angering the spirits. The result was that all women between fifteen and forty-five years were chronically anaemic because of lack of greens in their diet. If they caught pneumonia they would be dead in twelve hours. The missionary doctors practised a very effective form of preventive medicine: preaching Christ delivered women from the fear of offending the spirits, and an early reading primer urged on them the importance of eating green vegetables. The result was that soon healthy women were giving birth to healthy babies. It would be difficult to defend the idea that these people were all right as they were in their former state and that the missionaries were wrong to interfere with their culture and their taboos.

A world without Christ is a world full of fears and superstitions.

3. *Gratifying the cravings of our sinful nature* (verse 3)

This can happen in a primitive society. The tribe mentioned above was dying out, not only through disease on top of anaemia, but because of a venereally spread staphylococcus that caused sterility in women. In earlier days there had been a stricter sexual morality, but a breakdown in morals leading to widespread promiscuity, together with this disease, caused a sharp fall in the birthrate. Again the introduction of the Christian teaching on marital faithfulness effectively wiped out the disease.

Across the border in Sarawak (the East Malaysian part of Borneo), the government ban on head-hunting caused widespread male unemployment in another tribal group. (Missions interfere relatively little with cultures compared with government, insurrection movements, communism and foreign commercial interests.) It was not that they took many heads, but that previously they needed to keep sentry watch for marauding groups from other tribal groups. Now with time on their hands, they turned to alcohol: according to the *Sarawak Gazette* they could be drunk for a hundred days in the year, five days at a time, men, women and children, and so much so that babies died because their mothers were too drunk to suckle them. Are they really all right as they are? With disease and other problems, this Murut tribe (as they were then called) was fast dying out. Mercifully, the Christian gospel reached them from Indonesian Christians on the other side of the border, and they are now one of the most vigorous and fast-growing and progressive among the tribes. The whole tribe are now professing Christians.

It can happen also in sophisticated societies, as we know only too well. I remember a Singaporean woman, a university lecturer, weeping after an evangelistic service because her husband, a government official, was having an affair with his secretary. Marital unfaithfulness brings misery to the partner, and as is widely understood, to the children also. An extraordinary percentage of those in prison come from disturbed homes, and all schoolteachers know that the difficult children in class nearly always prove to have some major problem at home. In spite of this our society continues to make infedelity, denial of marriage vows, and sexual promiscuity the subject of novels, magazine stories, television drama and films without honestly exposing the suffering and spoiling of lives that inevitably result. By contrast the Christian standards are 'sound teaching', that is literally 'healthy words' (2 Timothy 1:13).

4. *We were by nature objects of wrath* (verse 3)
The Bible does speak of a future wrath of God at the time of final judgment (as in Romans 2:5), but the same letter earlier tells us that 'The wrath of God is being revealed from heaven against all the godlessness and wickedness of men who suppress the truth by their wickedness' (Romans 1:18). That is, that when we disobey God's laws, wittingly or unwittingly, our foolish actions have inevitable consecquences – as inevitable as the explosive effects of dropping water into concentrated sulphuric acid. The universe has been made that way – and so sexual promiscuity and marital infidelity produce misery and insecurity. Hatred and malice likewise produce bitterness and misery. Selfishness and greed result in cruelty and injustice. The daily newspapers and television broadcasts report on the outworking of this 'wrath' even though they do not present it in that way.

5. *We were dead in transgressions* (verse 5)
The most frustrating thing about the non-Christian world is the fact that huge populations never have the opportunity of even giving serious consideration to God's message in the Bible at all. Because of the presuppositions of the Hindu

29

and Buddhist world, even in theoretically secular states, it would be very difficult for those people to understand Christian teaching even if they were to have the opportunity of hearing it explained. In Islamic and Marxist states there is a huge government-backed conspiracy to suppress every Christian effort to give people the opportunity of hearing the Christian message at all. They are forced to live in a spiritual 'black-out'. They are not Muslims or Marxists by choice, but because they are not given the opportunity of considering any alternative world view, particularly not the Christian one (whatever the Declaration of Human Rights may say). They are thus described here as being living dead (verses 1–2). They are like the zombies of the Voodoo sects, walking corpses which give every appearance of life, but are in fact not genuinely alive at all, but animated by wicked forces. Thus the masses of pagan people* are 'dead' as far as their true Creator is concerned, and therefore need to be made alive as these verses describe. It is this spiritual deadness, blindness and darkness which the New Testament sees as being even more terrible than physical deprivation and injustice which are also a cause of deep concern to Christians.

But the writer returns to this theme of the need of people without Christ later in this passage, when he contrasts the deprivation of the Gentile nations with the privileges enjoyed by the Jews who did have a true revelation from God in the Old Testament.

6. *'Gentiles'* (verse 11)
The very expression translated 'Gentiles' or 'nations' was a derogatory one, whether used by Jews of the uncircumcised 'goyim' or by the Greeks of illiterate barbarians who could not speak Greek. The world without Christ is full of derogatory words for other ethnic groups – a world divided

* 'You' in verses 1–2 is contrasted with 'we' Jews with a knowledge of the true God in verse 3, and later verses 11–12.

by racial and tribal feuds and prejudices: words like wogs and gooks and honkies and niggers, Yanks and Limeys, frogs and Boche, Brits and poms. Only the Chinese are people – everyone else is a kind of foreign devil of some kind. In Taiwan they speak of the communist bandits on the mainland and the dwarf bandits in Japan. The world outside of Christ is a divided world full of racial hatred and ethnic rivalries. Can we honestly say that it is all right as it is?

7. *Without Messiah or 'separate from Christ'* (verse 12)
Both Jews and Christians see history as moving meaningfully towards a conclusion with the coming of the Messiah. But Gentile history is cyclical and pointless, like a book without a plot and without any conclusion. Buddhists and more philosophical Hindus see the world as an illusion (*maya* or *kuu*) on the TV screen of their sense organs, having no objective reality. In Japan a particularly nihilistic view among young people favoured three negatives – no interest, no response, no concern. Westerners in countries such as France have imbibed an existentialist outlook which sees life as absurd. The world without Christ is a world of pessimism and escapism. Is it really true that these people are all right as they are?

8. *Lacking any true corporate entity*
'Excluded from citizenship in Israel and foreigners to the covenants of the promise' (verse 12). Both Jews and Christians have a strong sense of corporate identity as 'the people of God'. The Christian doctrine of the church in which all Christians belong to one international brotherhood, irrespective of racial, social or sexual distinctions, is not actually unique. The Sikhs have a strong sense of brotherhood, and the brotherhood of Islam can also be meaningful. For philosophical Buddhists their own consciousness is the only reality, and the rest all illusion, so they live in subjective isolation from others. Yet others feel racial or national identity strongly. Indeed, Islam has a

31

strong doctrine of the state. Perhaps it is the Western world which is most adrift. The alienation of big cities and high-rise apartments, where every man is an island, causes extreme existential loneliness. But the detribalized growing cities of Africa are just as alienated. In the high-rise cities of Asia like Hong Kong, where the Chinese University researchers estimate that one person in three verges on clinical neurosis, there is deep alienation. There is in the heart of everyone a longing for true community, for the beautiful society. It was that which motivated the Khmer Rouge to destroy the fabric of the old society and drive the population from Phnom Penh into the countryside of Kampuchea, producing bitter disillusion and economic disaster for a whole nation. Is it really true that people divided and estranged from one another are all right as they are, without the gospel?

9. *'Without hope'* (verse 12)
The world without Christ is a world of despair and pessimism in the face of death. The fatalism of Islam, the teaching of illusion in Buddhism or reincarnation in Hinduism provide no permanently satisfying answer. What horror for the Thai when their loved ones die and become relentless evil spirits. What disillusion in the 'encouragement' that one's loved ones are only illusions anyway. The Japanese poet Issa loved his children, as any man does, but one by one they died until finally his much-loved, one surviving son died as well. His Buddhist friends came to comfort him, like some Japanese Job, reminding him that this was a transient world of dew. He replied with the famous poem:

Tsuyu no yo wa, tsuyu no yo nagara, sarinagara.
('The world of dew is a world of dew, and yet, and yet . . .')

thus expressing that most poignant human longing for survival after death, that our loved ones might be real and that we might meet again. What a privilege to preach 'we

32

believe that Jesus died and rose again and so we believe that God will bring with Jesus those who have fallen asleep in him' (1 Thessalonians 4:14). This Christian teaching about resurrection, reunion and new resurrection bodies* is particularly appreciated by leprosy sufferers. Missionary doctors and nurses treat their leprosy and do tendon transplant operations to restore mobility to their hands, while physiotherapists and then occupational therapists go on to help them regain their self-respect. But the prospect of new bodies, like Jesus' glorious body, is good news indeed to them. It is not insignificant, then, that in many countries the first people to turn to Christ have been deformed, disabled and sometimes despised people. When two Christian leprosy nurses were taken for ransom and subsequently found shot in Thailand, a former Muslim testified at their funeral to the love of Christ shown by these women who did not shrink from binding up his ulcerated feet and treating his leprosy.

The good news of Jesus then brings hope to people without hope in face of death. It is not that the Christian message teaches that the rain will descend, the floods rise and the wind blow on the house of the foolish who builds on sand, and that the sun will always shine for the wise man who builds on rock· for everyone faces the storms and disasters of life. But faith in Christ gives people strength and *hope* to withstand every onslaught.

10. *'Without God in the world'* (verse 12)
This certainly applies to those who worship false gods, whether in the affluent West or the underprivileged East. In the Zen Garden of the beautiful Ryoanji Temple in Kyoto, Japan, where people meditate on the rocks rising through the well-raked sand, like islands in the sea or mountain peaks through the clouds, they give you a translated handout which explains:

* Romans 8:23; 1 Corinthians 15:49; Philippians 3:21.

'Zen is a religion without god(s).
Zen is a religion without an object of worship.
Zen is a religion in which you worship yourself.'

Indeed what hope is there if my self is all the god there is in this world? Are such people really all right as they are?

The glorious good news

These sad descriptions of the state of people without Christ are set in a framework that tells us that God is rich in mercy and full of love for us, and that, because of his incomparable riches of grace and kindness, he has made us alive in Christ. But this salvation does not only result in blessing for individual sinners now made alive; it also brings them together (verse 19) as fellow-citizens with God's people and members of God's household. Christian longhouses in the tribes whose former miserable state I have described above wonderfully demonstrate this. Their life-style is very simple; they import only a few things from the outside world – cocoa powder, soap powder, outboard motors, transistor radios and the like. They don't yet have the blessing of television to tell them what else they are missing or make them dissatisfied. (Commercial interests never believe that people are all right as they are!) In the cool evening the old people sit on the benches along a quarter-mile long veranda, while the children skip with rattan and high-jump with bamboo. It looks like a fulfilment of Zechariah's prophecy: 'Once again men and women of ripe old age will sit in the streets of Jerusalem, each with cane in hand because of his age. The city streets will be filled with boys and girls playing there' (Zechariah 8:4–5). It's almost like a painting by Brueghel in which people come back from bathing in the swift-flowing river, carrying bananas, pineapples, fish, venison or wild boar for the evening meal. The old life of fear, superstition, taboos, disease and alcoholism had been replaced by a simple, almost idyllic life of contentment, community feeling, family love and staunch Christian faith. I asked the missionary whether, of 700 people living under one roof, there were not some nominal Christians among them. 'Well,' she replied, 'there are two or three we are not sure of!' What a privilege to have seen the transforming power of the gospel change whole communities in one missionary lifetime. The whole community had become a local church.

Perhaps I could conclude by telling you about two situations that left a deep impression on me. One concerns a Japanese person I got to know when I was first in Japan and my language very limited. This young man was a TB sufferer of around my own age who had taught himself English by listening to radio broadcasts. He was unable to work because of his illness and therefore was not entitled to any sick pay or insurance benefit. He felt he was a burden on his family who supported him as he lay weakly around at home while they paid for his treatment. One Christmas Eve the two of us walked out to a headland looking out over the wild waves of the Pacific, as the wind lashed us and snow came swirling down around us. It was a wild and beautiful sight. He stood looking down and said mournfully, 'This is the kind of place where we Japanese like to commit suicide . . .'

I pulled him away from the edge and homewards, realizing that for him everything seemed hopeless, and that suicide was the obvious Japanese option. How could anyone say that people are all right as they are, without Christ?

He did not come to faith then, nor for two or three years, but finally after a severe haemorrhage, dying, he called the missionary in to baptize him. And then he did not die after all, but slowly recovered. I remember vividly the day when he told me that the doctor had told him he could now get a job and even get married. Would I try to arrange a marriage for him? Well, we did, and even more vividly I remember the day when he was first introduced to a Christian girl who had steadfastly refused non-Christian suitors whom her family had repeatedly urged her to accept. It was quite a moment when they looked at each other for the first time. I would have to admit that my friend, after his long illness, was not the most handsome or prepossessing of men, and I think he was aware of this himself, for he looked at her in disarming fashion and said simply: 'If you don't think very much of me, it just shows that you did not pray as hard as I did!' (rather a nice compliment, implying that his own prayers had been abundantly answered).

We took part in their wedding ceremony, and down the years he has been a faithful elder in that local church. When we held the engagement service we read the words from Psalm 128, 'Blessed are all who fear the Lord, who walk in his ways. You will eat the fruit of your labour; blessings and prosperity will be yours. Your wife will be like a fruitful vine within your house; your sons will be like olive shoots round your table.' That had once seemed so improbable. But in due course two olive branches duly appeared, and when I last saw him in May 1980, he and his wife were driving their own car and looking quite prosperous, and he was still an active leader in the church.

If that was all I had ever done as a missionary, it would have been worth it just to see the change in that one man, when God made him alive in Christ. Often we speak of millions without Christ, but a million is just a million times one individual like that, and there are many more like him, waiting for someone to tell them about Christ.

The other I did not see with my own eyes, though I knew all the people involved – seven adults and ten children (and three unborn babies) on board a hospital van that crashed in central Thailand. In the wreck most were dead or dying, severely injured or unconscious. People came running. With the background of our Christian culture, we would expect that they were coming to help and comfort. But this was a country largely without Christ, and they came hurrying, not to succour, but to steal. The semi-conscious injured felt hands running over them searching pockets and bags.

36

That's what it means to live among people without Christ. That is why they need others to take the good news of Jesus to them.

Check: Think about the implications for people who have never had the opportunity to respond to the gospel, and pray about the implications of that for you.

Three
What do missionaries do?

Objectives:
To show from Acts that the main purpose of missionary work is to plant new churches where none exist and perfect existing churches where they do. All so-called 'specialized' groups are only ancillary to this main purpose, depend upon local churches themselves and will be judged eventually by the extent to which they have contributed to the growth of churches.

In the previous chapter, we saw what Christ does for people corporately. He brings them into membership of new communities of light and love, making them 'fellow-citizens with God's people and members of God's household' (Ephesians 2:19). Perhaps sometimes in the West we have lost sight of the importance of these basic Christian communities, and think that churches are merely incidental organizations within institutionalized Christianity. We think that the gospel tells how an individual may be saved. But the letter to the Ephesians declares that both individual salvation and the corporate community are essential parts of the gospel. The churches are not merely incidental means of grace to help individuals to be saved. They are not merely temporary providers of care and protection while we are on earth. God's long term purpose is to produce a new, beautiful, redeemed human society in which he himself will dwell.

What is missionary work all about?

This seems a glaringly obvious question, but I have found
from experience that even Christians who ought to know
better give a variety of vague and pious answers that fall
short of a full biblical answer. To do good, to preach the
gospel, to save souls, to heal the sick, to baptize bodies are
all good and true answers, but fall short of what stands out a
mile in the New Testament account in Acts. What did those
first apostolic missionaries like Paul, Barnabas, Silas and
Timothy actually do? Certainly they did preach and teach,
heal and serve – but why? For what purpose? Not just to
save individual souls. Acts is absolutely clear. They planted
churches.

Now this is something that needs emphasizing. We live
in a day of techniques, methodologies and specializations.
Enthusiastic individuals found new movements and
organizations specializing in evangelizing young people,
students or hospital patients: or provide useful services by
translating the Bible, flying aeroplanes, relieving famines,
broadcasting, helping refugees, printing and distributing
literature, or making a host of other excellent and worthy
contributions to the Christian cause. We should note that
most of these movements have arisen first in countries
where there is already an existing network of local churches
of various denominations. But we must never lose sight of
the fact that such organizations are only auxiliary, ancillary,
secondary and supplementary to the chief task of missions,
which is to *plant new churches*.

Unless we see this clearly, we shall be misled about the
nature of missionary work. It is obviously excellent that the
gospel should be preached by every possible means to all
sorts of people, and that tracts should be widely distributed
and every opportunity taken for witness. But we should not
think that by so doing we have necessarily accomplished
anything permanent and lasting. We know that for every
thousand tracts distributed, only a few will be read and

only a very few of those read in such a way as to bring people to faith in Christ. Again only a relatively small proportion of non-Christians ever get into Christian meetings at all, and only some of those get converted.

While all these specialized groups do a worthy work, then, they need to do it in such a way as to assist a solid church-planting work so that the growing church can nurture and build up those who may be reached by such methods. In recent years there has been a fresh realization that the local churches are the best soul-winning agencies there are.

This biblical emphasis on church-planting will also warn us of the grave limitations of short-term outreach in which young people spend a few weeks or months 'blitzing' an area with the gospel. This kind of service is excellent for training, for enabling young people to see the immensity of the need; but on its own it is an inadequate means of planting churches. Church-planting requires the patient work and steady slog of preaching, teaching disciples and building them together into viable self-propagating congregations. This requires the ability to speak and teach clearly in the local language, to understand and respond to problems created by the local culture, and that knowledge of people, places and situations that makes a Christian worker not only devoted, but relevant to the situation of people where they are. Above all, the church-planter needs to work in one place for an extended period of time.

So quite unequivocally I want to stress that missionary work must always centre on the local church – and that means that in pioneer areas, the primary, long-term task of missionaries must be to plant churches.

The biblical pattern

I have already asserted that this is what the apostles did. They planted churches. But you could well respond that Acts tells us about *individual* conversions – the man at the

Beautiful Gate, the Ethiopian, Saul of Tarsus, Cornelius, Lydia and the Philippian gaoler – and that only the last two of these are directly related to a new church being formed. So let me begin a review of Acts with all this in mind:

While the word 'church' is used only twice in the Gospels, in Acts it appears some nineteen times.

In *Jerusalem* 5:11; 8:1–3; 11:22; 12:1–5; 15:4–22.

In *Judea, Galilee and Samaria* 9:31 ('the church throughout').

In *Antioch* (Syria) 11:26; 13:1; 14:27; 15:3.

In *Galatia* 14:23 (Antioch, Iconium, Lystra, Derbe and Perga).

In *Syria and Cilicia* 15:41 (of which we know only of Antioch, Damascus, Tyre and Tarsus).

In *'the churches'* generally, 16:5.

In *Caesarea* 18:22.

In *Ephesus* 20:17–28.

So the man at the Beautiful Gate would have belonged to the church in Jerusalem, and Cornelius and his friends were presumably the nucleus of a new church in Caesarea mentioned in Acts 18:22.

The origin of the churches in Samaria must have been Philip's mission, and the early preaching of Peter and John (Acts 8:25). Later we find Peter visiting 'the saints in Lydda' (9:32) in Judea; 'the disciples' in the port of Joppa (9:38, including Dorcas and Simon the Tanner) and then initiating the Gentile work in the Roman garrison city of Caesarea (chapters 10 and 21). Later we know there was a church there (18:22) and Philip the evangelist among them (21:8), while further up the coast at Ptolemais there were 'brothers' and at Tyre 'the disciples' (21:4–7). After the church in Syrian Antioch was established (11:20ff.), Paul's first missionary journey to Cyprus and Galatia with Barnabas saw the four churches in Phrygia and Lycaonia established, and possibly also in Perga in Pamphylia (14:25). Then after revisiting the Galatian churches, Paul went on through Troas, this time with Silas, and planted new congregations in Philippi, Thessalonica and Berea, and subsequently in Athens and Corinth. The next great area opened up by Paul was Ephesus and the other cities of the province of Asia. Thus, while Luke was concerned about other matters including the charges brought against Paul in the closing chapters of the book, his account of evangelism is about the planting of churches, the starting of new congregations.

The centrality of church-planting

Church-planters are the infantry of God's army: there may be more colourful groups of cavalry, commandos, artillery, signals, engineers and ordnance, but they all exist to serve the main body so that they can win the battles. What does a radio evangelism work achieve if there are no churches to follow up their contacts and to help finance the programmes? What does a literature programme achieve if there are no churches to distribute their evangelistic literature or Christians to buy and read their books? Who follows up evangelistic work among students, if not the churches in which those students, graduating after three or four short years, will be nurtured for the rest of their lives? You cannot be in one of these ancillary ministries for very long without realizing how dependent you are on the existence of sympathetic local churches. After some years in Japan I was seconded by the Overseas Missionary Fellowship to work with KGK, the Japanese evangelical student fellow-ship. The strength of student Christian Unions in provincial universities depended on local churches which would pro-vide founder members, local pastors to help in teaching and most of all healthy sound fellowship in which new converts could be nurtured. This was equally true in the major cities.

Indeed, the value of all such 'para-church' or 'inter-denominational' work must always depend upon and be measured by the degree to which it helps to build and strengthen the local churches. There is two-way traffic certainly, but it is the local churches which are the ultimate biblical goal, and not the para-church organizations for their own sake.

Paul's church-planting in Corinth

Paul's work in Corinth gives a good illustration of what church-planting involves. We gain a picture of it by reading not only Acts 18, but also the Corinthian Epistles. Paul had two initial means of contact: his need to work, and his ethnic (and religious) affinity with the Jewish community. His need to support himself, through his trade of tent-making, brought him immediately into contact with Aquila and Priscilla, Jews from Pontus in Asia Minor, who shared his skill of making tents from the skins of black Cilician goats. The fact that they are initially called 'Jews' and *not* 'disciples' suggests that they must have become Christians in Corinth through their lodger. Later Paul's ministry was reinforced by the arrival of Silas of Jerusalem, another Roman citizen, and Timothy of Lystra who was half-Greek.

Paul's link with the Jewish community was made through the synagogue, which he always made the first point of contact with Jews and 'Godfearers' who knew the Scriptures. Crispus, the ruler of the synagogue, was converted with his whole household and baptized by Paul. This precipitated Paul's ejection from the synagogue, so that he moved next door to the house of Titus (or Titius) Justus, a Godfearing Gentile. Since the Romans had three names this nomen and cognomen went together with the praenomen Gaius, whom Paul called host (Romans 16:23) and whom he also baptized (1 Corinthians 1:14). It seems probable that the Sosthenes, whose name appears with Paul's in the salutation of the first letter (1 Corinthians 1:1), was Crispus' successor, who was also converted.

Paul also baptized the household of Stephanas (1 Corinthians 1:15; 16:15) among the first converts and we also know of the household of Chloe (1:11) and Fortunatus and Achaichus (16:17). At some point Phoebe the deacon (*diakonos*) and patroness (*prostatis*) of Cenchrea, the nearby port, must also have come to Christ. Thus we know of ten names, and in addition the five families or households of Aquila, Stephanas, Crispus, Chloe and probably Gaius. Church-planting today involves the same patient winning of individuals and their families, and their baptism and integration into the newly emerging congregation.

At one stage Paul was discouraged and fearful of the opposition, and may have contemplated pulling out, as he had done in Athens when there were only a few converts (Acts 17:34). But the Lord encouraged him in a vision, telling him not to be afraid, promising that he need not fear attack 'because I have many people in this city' (18:10).

It is this realization that God has a purpose for a locality which is so encouraging. Jeremiah's instructions to the exiles to 'seek the peace and prosperity of the city to which I have carried you into exile. Pray to the Lord for it, because if it prospers, you too will prosper' (29:7) remind us of this concern as do the words of the Lord Jesus to stay at some worthy person's house and 'let your peace rest on it' (Matthew 10:11–14). For Paul this is exactly what seems to have happened, first in the home of Aquila and Priscilla and then in the home of Gaius Titus Justus. So also the prophets brought blessing with them wherever they stayed (for example Elijah in the home of the widow of Zarephath (1 Kings 17). Paul stayed on in Corinth for eighteen months more, teaching the Christians.

That time in Corinth was productive in a different sense, for Paul was brought before the proconsul Gallio (who is known from an inscription found at Delphi to have been appointed by the Emperor Claudius in July AD 51). Gallio's court ruling created a legal precedent which acknowledged that Christian belief, like Judaism, was a *religio licita* in the eyes of Roman law.

Models

What happens in one situation may become a significant precedent over a much wider area, not only legally, but in a wider sense. Paul told the Thessalonians, 'you became a model to all the believers in Macedonia and Achaia' (1 Thessalonians 1:7). The Thessalonian church's growth, evangelism and firmness in the face of persecution was a stimulus, spur and pattern to other newly emerging congregations at that time. A local church can be significant, not only for its own sake, but as a model, a pattern church for other groups of Christians. The work done in one place sparks off action elsewhere. The work in Corinth seems to have sparked off something in Cenchrea. Paul's work in Ephesus later seems also to have produced other churches in the province of Asia like Colossae, Laodicea and Hierapolis.

Dr John Laird, a former General Secretary of the Scripture Union, used to warn people not to spread themselves too thinly by trying to do too much over too wide an area. Rather the worker should seek prayerfully to establish a pattern, in a limited area which others could then take as their model. We may know of such models in church history – in England Richard Baxter visiting in Kidderminster, or William Grimshaw saving souls at Haworth. We could suggest many contemporary model churches known to us – Coral Ridge, Florida; All Souls, London: or Gilcomston South, Aberdeen. There are great third-world models also. Festo Kivengere said that the home village of William Nagenda, one of the leaders of the East African revival, was noteworthy not only because it was full of converted people, but because the whole life-style of the community was significantly different from that of other villages in the district. Christian conviction raised the whole quality of life of the community.

This pattern of the local victory which becomes significant over a much wider area is well illustrated by Jonathan's success (1 Samuel 14) against a small outpost garrison which the Philistines had established in the pass at Michmash. Jonathan demonstrates initiative, example and the ability to involve others. But also it was an act of faith when Jonathan, with one of the two precious swords, and his unarmed armourbearer, climbed up to face a numerically much superior force. They trusted that the Lord could act whether by many or by few. They won the engagement, a relatively small skirmish in itself, in which they killed twenty of the invading force in a small area of ground. This sparked off a much bigger engagement, as the Lord caused the enemy to panic and Saul and his forces joined in the rout of the Philistines. Cowed and intimidated Israelites came out of their hiding places to join in as well.

A small local initiative of faith can spark off great blessing. Revivals often start in small insignificant places like Kilsyth in Scotland or Bario in the highlands of Borneo. So we should never undervalue the significance of our local engagement with the forces of evil, as we seek to build a congregation that is beautiful and credible. What happens to each of us really matters. The work done in one local church can become a significant pattern for the rest of the Christian world. Do not imagine that your labour for the Lord will ever be wasted.

Great Christian principles have to be demonstrated and worked out in local situations. Arm's-length Christianity, the 'Gospel Blimp' syndrome that makes us prefer big organization and committees to straightforward talking to people over the garden fence or in the street is little use. The Japanese have a nice expression, 'nikai no mekusuri', which means, 'eye medicine from the second floor': you can imagine using an eyedropper from that height! Real faith must be demonstrated at close quarters in the local situation. The power of the gospel has to be demonstrated at the local level and to be seen to have power to save there. If countries are to be evangelized, it will be by establishing convincing, credible local congregations, starting first in larger centres, and then pivoted on those, working out to smaller towns and villages.

What does church-planting involve?

It means starting in a town or district where there is no existing church, making contacts, developing friendships, leading people to faith in Christ, instructing converts, baptizing them, beginning church meetings with them and building them up into a functioning congregation in such a way that you can see local leaders trained and appointed, who will be able to carry on without you, and then moving on and starting the process all over again somewhere else. This is the pattern we have seen in Paul's work in Corinth and Ephesus.

It demands great patience and perseverance, and above all faith that God will work and that will not be weakened by any discouragements. Because Barnabas was full of faith (Acts 11:24) 'a great number of people were brought to the Lord'.

I remember one missionary who was especially good at fostering relationships with people that he met every day. So the first person to become a Christian was a postman, the second a milkman, the third a barber and the next a carpenter, to be followed by a plasterer, a rice merchant, a fireman and so on. You can see that it is not merely academic theological knowledge or powerful preaching which is needed. The church-planter is somebody who can work well in unstructured situations, who has the gift of making friends, getting alongside other people, and loving them. He will engage in house-to-house visiting, chatting to strangers in the market, open-air preaching and tract distribution, all aimed at bringing people into touch with a Christian meeting. Church-planting needs an infectious faith that can lead others to join with the missionary in seeking to bring yet others to faith, by reproducing yourself so that new Christians also gain the same passion for soul-winning. It is the most satisfying and rewarding work, the most useful and fruitful way of spending a life.

Rate of growth

In Java a recently started Bible College expects each one of its students to plant a new local congregation of at least thirty baptized believers before they are allowed to graduate! This does suggest that the area must be very responsive to the gospel: but what a marvellous way to train Christian workers as church-planters! By contrast, in countries which are very resistant like Islamic Bangladesh or pagan France, it may take many years, perhaps a whole lifetime, to build a single congregation. Where people are responsive it may be possible to start a new congregation every year as one friend of mine did in Metropolitan Manila, or even to pioneer a number of different congregations all at the same time.

When a new vital congregation has formed it is probably a mistake to over-consolidate that initial church fellowship and concentrate merely on putting up a building, where-upon all growth ceases, physically limited thereafter by the walls that have been erected around it. I remember being present in a Sarawak longhouse when the Christian meeting place was too small for all who wanted to gather, and being delighted to see someone get a hammer and knock down a partition so that we would have more room. The Nevius Indigenous Policy in Korea meant that instead of being dependent on foreign mission-board funds to supply a permanent building, several committees and two years later, they used their own simple buildings, and when they became too small, demolished a wall and extended it in time for the next week's service.

Every growing church should be encouraged to start early in pioneering a new daughter congregation nearby. It is much easier for an existing congregation to allocate a group of its members as the nucleus of a new work, than for a foreign missionary to have to start from scratch all on his own. However, a combination of the two, with the missionary assisting the national Christians in spearheading new evangelistic outreach, is probably the most effective approach of all. A congregation started in post-war Tokyo by a widowed American missionary lady in her sixties, now has no less than five daughter congregations. In Bangkok one missionary-pioneered congregation pioneered a second, and then the two congregations each started their own daughter congregation: this repeated doubling of congregations promises the most effective growth and penetration of the community.

In Singapore the oldest Christian Brethren assembly (founded in 1862) founded two new daughter congregations in the 1970s yet it is still packed to the doors, with no less than 80% of its membership having been baptized in the last five years. This is partly because young people, though converted in a city-centre church, have to move out to suburban Housing Development Board flats for financial reasons when they get married. These young couples form the nucleus of the new congregations. Another Bible Church group bought a new suburban house each year for several successive years, allowing a young couple to live upstairs and a new congregation to start meeting on the ground floor. This rapid growth is most thrilling.

These I would call 'sweet divisions' which are deliberate and planned, and prayed for, in contrast to situations where churches become stagnant and frustrated so that in the end some personality conflict brings them to a 'bitter division', which is in reality a sad split and a denial of their unity in Christ.

One of the problems is how to deploy missionaries to best advantage. In view of the considerable cost of supporting a missionary family, it could be argued that it is wiser to deploy missionaries in areas where churches can be planted most rapidly, than to spend a missionary lifetime planting just one church in a resistant area. It is obviously better to put missionaries where they can start ten congregations in twenty or thirty years, than in places where they plant only one in thirty years. This is probably true in countries like Japan or Thailand where the population-drift to the large cities means that new groups in the more traditional countryside with its shrines and temples grow very slowly compared with those in urban areas with a constant influx of new people, usually with minimal religious loyalties. In resistant countries, however, somebody has to shed blood, sweat and tears to get the first bridgehead congregation established no matter how long it takes. The early struggles in Nepal in the fifties and sixties, when converts were few and many of them were imprisoned, were necessary to the present rapid growth of the church, doubling in membership annually in recent years. This is true also of Bangladesh, as Phil Parshall tells us in his book. * So you cannot really plan to put missionaries only where the work will be 'successful' – the motivation is all wrong: God is glorified wherever Christ is faithfully preached even if nobody will listen.

Strategy for closed resistant countries

Some closed countries can be reached by so-called 'tent-maker' missionaries – in other words committed Christians who can gain entry, not as overt missionaries but as business people, diplomats, medical workers and teachers. Other countries are closed even to them. Moreover the enormous social pressure put on people who turn to Christ makes evangelism very difficult. It is then that we see the value of church-planting work overseas among students, immigrant labourers, resettled refugees, expatriate business communities and small enclaves from resistant provinces in more open capital cities.

For example, there are thriving Chinese churches all over Europe and North America. There are Japanese con-

* Philip Parshall, *New Paths in Muslim Evangelism* (Baker Book House, 1980).

gregations made up entirely of business people in cities like Dusseldorf, Singapore, London, Bonn and Bangkok, where they seem much more open to the gospel than they are in their homeland. Again, though Kampuchea is very difficult at present, there has been a very effective work in the refugee camps along the Thai border. In other places there are Tibetan and Afghan refugees, and work in their homelands is almost impossible. The Kurds are a stateless people living mainly in an area covering parts of Turkey, Iran, Iraq and the USSR – all lands closed to missions. There are twenty million of them, with few known Christians among them. Yet among the Turkish migrant workers in Germany there are many Kurds who can be reached with the gospel. There are Arab and other Islamic states where government policies and social pressure make it difficult for people to have any free choice or opportunity seriously to consider the Christian faith. But expatriate Muslims, outside that situation, may well be much more open to consider the claims of the Lord Jesus carefully.

Students should not be disregarded either, for though church-planting in some hostile Muslim countries may not seem possible or sensible, many have found Christ while studying overseas. Several years ago six or seven Malay students were converted in Europe. There is, however, always a problem for such temporary exiles when they return home again, and the social pressure against open confession of Christ is so overwhelming that, in the absence of supporting congregations of believers, they may turn away from the Lord or backslide.

The long-term significance of church-planting

The church needs to evangelize, and slogans like 'Evangelize to a finish to bring back the King' or 'The speediest evangelization of Asia's millions' are fine as far as they go. Such slogans seem to me inadequate, however, because they fail to reflect the biblical emphasis on the church. I feel

51

much happier with the concept of 'a church in every community'. In the New Testament, while the saving of individuals is significant, it is so because such evangelism is a necessary part of planting churches. You cannot plant churches without evangelizing, but you can evangelize without bringing new congregations into being. I am not implying that para-church organizations which specialize in particular forms of evangelism are necessarily misguided. But I am saying that they should not see their ministries as an end in themselves, but as valuable only to the extent to which they help to strengthen existing churches and to plant new ones.

A local church which is functioning properly* is a community of God's people in which those who are evangelized by 'specialist' agencies may be nurtured, trained, disciplined, shepherded and ministered to. The individual convert without the backing of the local church may grow cold, backslide, stray into doctrinal error or fall into moral sin. These things can befall church members also, as we well know; but if the congregation is functioning properly there is much more hope that they will be spiritually warmed, helped forward, taught to maintain the truth, and, if not kept from sin, admonished with such love and grace that they are quickly restored again.

The local church is also part of the universal church, and though entire local churches, whole denominations and even churches on a national scale may be virtually wiped out by persecution, apostasy and heresy, God is always at work through his Spirit to quicken and renew his church. And just as the family strengthens the individual, providing a secure base for identity, so also the local congregation provides a secure caring community for the preservation and strengthening of the individual believer.

* See the extended treatment in the author's two books, *Cinderella with Amnesia* (IVP, 1975, also published as *God's Forgetful Pilgrims* by Eerdmans) and *Shaking the Sleeping Beauty* (IVP, 1980, also published as *The Church and World Mission* by Zondervan).

The implications for you

What we have been saying, of course, is not only significant for missionaries or full-time ministers of the gospel. Every single one of us, if we are committed Christian men or women, has a responsibility to work and serve within that Christian community. We shall also be concerned to see that the church continues to grow and to go out in evangelism. We shall never be satisfied with maintaining a church at its existing size, but ever concerned for fresh outreach and the planting of new daughter congregations.

And if we are called by the Lord, and by his church, to full-time service, then we shall always hold this goal of church-planting before us. When we consider which missionary society to join, we shall want to know whether that particular fellowship is committed to church-planting or merely to maintaining an existing institutional structure for its own sake. If we consider serving with a para-church agency – many of them excellent bodies used by God for his glory – we shall want to know whether they are free-lance agencies which just do what is right in their own eyes, or whether they relate to existing local churches and through their work directly or indirectly contribute to the planting of new ones.

A friend of mine who has for many years led student work in the Philippines, and throughout East Asia, recently attained a lifelong ambition – to become a pastor in a local church in Manila. He has always seen that the ministry of planting and perfecting churches is the crucial and primary task to which we are committed. Let me quote from an article which he wrote, expressing this so very well:

As a community of believers, such new men demonstrate in their relationships to each other what is best for society as a whole. Justice, equality, human dignity, help for the needy – each of these is so abstract until given flesh and bones in daily human relationships. The wider

53

community needs a living model: *the Christian community must be that model.* And, as the example is set, the whole community ethic will be raised by the sheer power of moral influence.

(Isabelo Magalit, *OIL*, March 1971)

The local church is the essential basic unit of any long-lasting Christian strategy.

Check: What place does the local church play in your Christian life now?

Do you see building up congregations into credible and beautiful communities as a worthwhile task for the whole of your life?

Do you test the value of all missionary work by the criterion of the extent to which they fulfil this purpose?

Four
What will it cost?

Objectives:
*To show that Christian discipleship involves sacrifice and a willing-
ness to lose our lives for the sake of the gospel. To identify with other
races in order to win them for Christ may involve the costly sacrifice of
a comfortable Western life-style.*

To many people, and often even more to their families, the
prospect of becoming a missionary seems a recklessly foolish
and wasteful sacrifice. Today there is still some element of
sacrifice, but we must not think of it in an irrationally
sensational or sentimentally exaggerated way; we must
think of it in a biblical way. There is no point in taking risks
or making sacrifices unless it is clear that Jesus Christ
commands it, and that our sacrifice has a proper biblical
and theological foundation.

In Luke chapter 9 we are told how Jesus took his disciples
up to the very north of Israel, to Caesarea Philippi where
the sources of the Jordan river spring out of the foothills of
Mt Hermon. There where the trout still move through the
rippling waters, and far away from the crowds, Jesus
questioned his disciples about himself: 'Who do the crowds
say I am?' and 'Who do you say I am?' And Peter makes his
famous confession that Jesus is the Messiah of God (Luke
9:20). The first half of Jesus' teaching, concerning who he

55

was, was completed. 'From that time on Jesus began to explain to his disciples that he must go to Jerusalem and suffer many things...he must be killed and on the third day be raised to life' (Matthew 16:21). This is the second great lesson, and concerns the work Jesus had come to do.

Having first spoken of his own suffering and death, Jesus goes on to say that those who follow him as disciples must also be ready to suffer: the disciple must deny himself and take up his cross daily and follow Jesus (Luke 9:23ff.). If the teacher and Lord suffers, so also must his followers. Then Jesus explains a basic principle essential to our understanding of this aspect of missions:

> For whoever wants to save his life will lose it,
> but whoever loses his life for me will save it (Luke 9:24).

There are two sorts of people among us: one sort wishes to preserve their life in security and comfort, avoiding self-denial or risk of martyrdom; the other is willing to risk everything, as Jesus says, 'for me'. You must be willing to lose it all – your prospects of wealth, or comfort, or marriage, or eminence, or success – all for Jesus' sake. In so doing we are not only following his example, but also being moved and motivated by it: he suffered for us, and we must therefore be willing to suffer for him.

Now this idea of being willing to 'lose' suggests the 'losses' we may anticipate in becoming a missionary. Paul's letter to the Philippians speaks almost in passing about the sacrifices or losses which he experienced in his missionary service. We shall look at them one by one:

1. Loss of cultural privilege and status
2. Loss of standard of living
3. Loss of security and health
4. Loss of family and friends
5. Loss of life itself

As disciples of Jesus we are required to be prepared to risk such losses. And if we do, we shall find that instead of losing out or being penalized we shall in fact have saved our lives, and been immeasurably enriched.

1. *Cultural privilege and status*

In Philippians 3:7 Paul says that all his seeming assets and credits had become losses and debits 'for the sake of Christ'. Many things in which he could take pride within his own Jewish culture meant little or nothing on the Gentile mission field. The proud intellectual Greeks of Athens would probably not think much of the Turkish university of Tarsus, and still less of the rabbinic schools of Jerusalem. They had probably never heard of Gamaliel, the rabbi at whose feet Paul had studied and of whom he was so proud. To the Gentiles, Paul's Jewish pedigree and his Jewish education described in Philippians 3:5 meant nothing. This is part of the price which every missionary has to pay when he moves from his own culture into another one: his cultural assets are frozen, and his privileges become disadvantages.

I remember preaching on the street one cold freezing day in Hirosaki, in Northern Japan. I offered a tract to a peasant girl from the country, and I curled up inside when she spurned me and refused the leaflet. I remember feeling: 'Doesn't she know that I am a graduate of Cambridge University?' She did not know, and even if she had, it would have meant nothing to her. All your academic assets, cultural credits and intellectual pride lose their value when you cross over into another culture.

There is a Japanese missionary working with the Overseas Missionary Fellowship in Thailand. In Japan he would have been much respected, for his grandfather had been a famous professor of law at Tokyo University and a teacher of several Prime Ministers. His father was a well-known journalist. In Thailand he is just one more foreign missionary, and his distinguished name means nothing to the Thais or even to his fellow-missionaries. His six years in university, three years' theological training and years of

57

church experience mean nothing now as he struggles to learn and speak the Thai language. The prestige that was once gain to him has been lost.

There is the sacrifice of freedom to express oneself in one's own language, and to hold people's attention with eloquent explanations. It doesn't matter how skilful you were once in your own native language, all that has to be left behind. We have already seen that you have to be born again once more, this time as a cultural infant, a linguistic idiot. You cannot make yourself understood and you cannot understand what others say. Like a baby you can only smile and make hopeful noises which nobody understands, while your adult personality cringes with embarrassment. Other people say things to you, and you can only nod politely and hope they don't discover that you cannot make head or tail of what they are saying. A congregation splits its sides with laughter, but the joke is quite beyond you, and you can only grin weakly.

But some things do carry over. I think of a Maori missionary from New Zealand, also working in Thailand among peasant farmers in the Muslim south. He did impress the farmers because he could stay on an untamed horse and could skin and cut up a cow faster than any of them could! But a PhD or a theological doctorate would not have impressed them in the least.

In Jerusalem Paul had been regarded as a promising young scholar. He wrote, 'I was advancing in Judaism beyond many Jews of my own age' (Galatians 1:14). He had a great future and was emerging as a leader of the Pharisees, the purest and most committed and godly group in Israel. But now in Greece he is regarded as a nobody, and 'the scum of the earth' (1 Corinthians 4:13). Being a Christian meant for him, as it means for us, being ready to turn our backs on the recognition we might have achieved in our own society.

It's not surprising if you are reluctant to leave your own home country to become a missionary. At home you are somebody. You are known and appreciated. You have a place in society through your family and friends. What is the loss that the Lord Jesus asks you to face? Never mind if you are *somebody* at home. Are you willing to become a *nobody* in some far distant place where no-one knows you? That is the risk he asks us to take: and it is this loss of the life we have enjoyed till now that we fear.

Think for a moment of young Joseph, secure in his father's love and proud of his father's gift of the long-sleeved coat of many colours. Now his cultural coat is stripped off him, he suffers the indignity of being sold as a despised foreign slave in Egypt and is thrown into prison. Will he succeed in his new situation? Will he just crumble away in defeat and despair, or does he have faith in God to help him start all over again in this new country? It's a wonderful story of faith and how God was with him there.

Are you willing to lose your cultural coloured coat, to be torn from your family and friends, to start all over again in a strange country and to be thrown into the prison of language learning, unable to communicate any more? This is part of the risk that the Lord asks us to take – to lose our present life, and to join with him in the adventure of starting all over again.

He has done something like it himself, only much more so. Philippians 2:5–11 describes how he left his Father's throne and sapphire-paved courts, heaven where the angels worshipped him, in order to 'start all over again' as a human infant, helpless and dependent, born in a stable and learning to work with his own hands as a humble country carpenter. That is why he has the right to ask us to do what he has himself already done for our sake. He emptied himself, he humbled himself. He asks us to be willing to do the same.

2. *Standard of living*
In Philippians 4:11–12 Paul claims that he is content in any and every circumstance and that he has learned the secret

of being full and being hungry. He is used to an irregular supply of funds: sometimes he has plenty, often he has little. He writes of serving God 'in beatings, imprisonments and riots; in hard work, sleepless nights and hunger' and of being 'poor, yet making many rich; having nothing, and yet possessing everything' (2 Corinthians 6:5, 10).

Jesus asks us to be willing to lose the affluence and prosperity in which we have grown up. He asks us to be prepared to accept relative poverty, and move from a high standard of living to a much simpler life-style. This is not easy. We may not be like the people Paul describes in Philippians 3:19 ('their god is their stomach'), but we do enjoy the comforts of life.

Some missionaries appear in the Third World like invaders from Mars! They live in their own space-capsule with air-conditioning and filtered water, eat expensively imported western food and keep themselves isolated from the jostling crowds by means of air-conditioned motor cars. Just occasionally they don their space suits to give out tracts and take prisoners. They are usually ineffective except for attracting people who hope to get some material benefits out of them. I remember an Indian friend talking about a group of western evangelists who took their own bottled water with them to India. 'What's wrong with our Indian water?' he asked indignantly, 'you can boil it like any other water. I want a missionary who will drink with me out of the same dirty tap!' But you reply that you have always been used to drinkable tap water, a refrigerator, washing machine, television, sleeping in a bed, and, of course, your own car! You could not possibly give up these things to become a missionary.

Why not? He who tries to save his life will lose it.

In the jungles of Borneo there are no roads at all. Either you go by plane or you walk. One hour in the plane is two weeks' walk. In rural Thailand the narrow paths between rice paddies will take motor bikes but not cars. That Japanese missionary I mentioned would have had a decent vehicle back home in Japan. But I remember clinging beside him on the back of a little local bus (there was no room inside), coughing and spluttering in the dust. As missionaries we watch the wealthy western tourists come out of luxury hotels into their air-conditioned coaches, while we sweat past pedalling our bicycles in the tropical heat. We eat the local diet while they stuff themselves with luxuries. The tourist passes over the surface of the culture as though in a glass-bottomed boat. The real missionary has got to learn to swim in the cultural water. And that means accepting the ordinary living standards of the people he lives with. And of course they will not notice that he is making any sacrifice, will they? He is sharing their ordinary daily life.

I looked at a missionary's house in the south of Thailand. It was a hovel. When you emptied a washing bowl in the bathroom, the water ran away in a gutter across the living room floor. It was a time when funds were short; the food allowance had been cut by 10% and the personal allowance by 50%. But by local standards he seemed a rich man nonetheless, and nobody saw any sacrifice in his living as they lived.

Are you willing to pay this price and sacrifice your living standards if necessary, and to be content with living like the people you are trying to reach with the gospel?

Why should we live simply? Because we need to get as close to people as we can. Even in more developed countries a rich missionary creates problems. I remember a GI friend of mine telling me that in Vietnam one of the problems of being a GI was that there was always a group of parasitic people around you trying to get things from you. It's just the same with missionaries if they have too much money and too many gadgets.

How can the Lord Jesus ask us to accept such loss and deprivation? Because he himself left the comfort of heaven to live in a poor Third World country: he walked the dusty roads, endured the hot winds from the desert. He knew sweat, flies, mosquitoes, lice and fleas.

3. *Security and health*

Paul is writing from an Eastern European prison (Philippians 1:13–14). Ancient prisons were not like our modern de luxe establishments; more like the horrible place in 'Midnight Express'. He had been in prison before in Philippi itself. Beaten, cast into the stocks, he and Silas could not run away when the earthquake occurred. Had God forgotten them? Was it all a dreadful divine oversight? No. God wanted them right there. We must realize that God is not interested primarily in our comfort and security but rather in blessing people through us (and incidentally blessing us at the same time). It was through Paul and Silas's suffering in jail that the gaoler was converted.

Why face the risk of going to countries which are politically insecure with the possibility of revolution, riots and war? Because God wants us there to bless people who are going through much suffering.

There was a most remarkably fruitful work in the city of Phnom Penh in Cambodia (now Kampuchea) before it fell to the Khmer Rouge. The city was crowded with refugees who swelled it to four times its normal population. Three out of four people were living in tents and shanties. Rockets were falling on the city. Many things were unobtainable and you had to pay a high price for the few things you could buy. The missionaries had to share in the suffering and the dangers of that doomed city. But in two years the church grew from 500 Christians to 5,000, a ten-fold growth. In Philippians we read that Epaphroditus was sick to the point of death and that this was due to his work for Christ, for whom he gambled or risked his life (2:26, 30). Like those missionaries in Phnom Penh, he staked his life.

Missionary work often means risking unpleasant diseases, mad dogs with rabies, mosquitoes, malaria and dengue fever, the freezing winters of Korea and Japan or the steaming humidity of the never-ending tropical summer where you never feel cool even at night and your clothes are always damp and sweaty. I was once or twice privileged to climb mountain trails with missionaries to the Philippine tribes. Your face is running with sweat and your shirt is soaked with it, you wade across river after river and you arrive to find leeches sucking your blood, a dozen or more like swollen black grapes between your toes and hanging from your ankles. I remember a Singaporean Chinese girl who went as a missionary to Pakistan. She faced humiliation and manhandling in the bazaars, and once was stoned because Chinese were politically unpopular. Are we prepared to pay this price of risking our security and hazarding our health in order to win men and women for Christ?

Look at the risks the Lord Jesus took when he was born as a human baby in an insanitary cave-stable, full of germs and the smell of dung and urine. He could so easily have died of infection. He chose to live upon the lowest point of the earth's surface – the lake of Galilee is 695 feet below sea level, and along the Jordan valley which runs down to the Dead Sea, 1285 feet below sea level. Is it not astonishing that he chose to live in stifling heat in the deepest trench on the earth's surface?

He can ask us to take risks because he took the most enormous risks on our behalf.

4. *Family and friends*

Paul says, 'I consider everything a loss' (Philippians 3:8), probably meaning that he was disowned by his Jewish family in Tarsus. Other apostles might have the right to take with them a wife (1 Corinthians 9:5) and there were women workers on Paul's team (Philippians 4:3), but it would have been a very tough itinerant life for any woman to share. Timothy had left his own dear mother and grandmother behind in Lystra in order to serve with Paul as a son with a father (Philippians 2:22). Missionary work meant then, as it still often does now, frequent moves from place to place and the lack of a secure permanent home. This is probably that part of the cost of missionary work from which many of us shrink back most. The Lord may ask us to leave our home and family and friends.

I can still remember sailing out of Southampton harbour on a Dutch ship twenty-five years ago, heading for the Far East for the first time. Leaning over the ship's side we could converse with my father and my wife's parents who were standing on the quay-side. Then as the ship began very slowly to pull away, through our tears we could see them very slowly receding from us. As we pulled further and further out, and tugs blew their hooters, the figures of our loved ones became smaller and smaller until we could just see them give a final wave and walk away.

We have no *right* to stay with our parents, to marry or to have children. These are special privileges and rich human joys. But if we seek first those things then we may fail to seek first his kingdom and his righteousness. In his love and mercy he often throws those things in again as a bonus when we seek first of all his kingdom.

There is the loneliness of the unmarried. A Japanese poet wrote a moving little poem about a single missionary lady:

'Dendoo no tame ni, hitori sumu Missu Howardo,
Yofuke, hikido ni joo orosu kage...'

which roughly translated means, 'For the sake of the gospel, living alone Miss Howard, late at night locking the sliding door, her shadow....' Miss Howard was a good soul-winner who led many to Christ, but this verse catches the loneliness of her life. As the poet cycled home late at night all he could see of her was her shadow behind the frosted glass as she locked herself in. He wondered why anyone would choose to endure such loneliness. For the sake of the gospel.

On a more personal note, I remember hugging my six-year-old son at the Tokyo railway terminus and turning away so that he could not see my eyes filled with tears. It is just not practical for all missionaries to camp around foreign

64

schools so that their children can come home to sleep every night. If the children are to have proper schooling in their own language and enjoy the company of children of their own age, there will be the hurt of separation. Missionaries love their children just as much as anybody else, perhaps all the more because spending time with them is a special privilege. It is part of the loss that has to be faced.

How can the Lord Jesus ask such a price? He left his heavenly home, he was misunderstood by his earthly brothers; when dying on the cross he handed his mother over to the care of the apostle John. His friends forsook him and fled. He knows what human loneliness feels like. He knows what we do not know, the loneliness of the cross when he cried out, 'My God, my God, why have you forsaken me . . . ?' Yes, he can ask even the price of separation from parents, friends and children.

5. *Life itself*

We have already seen that Epaphroditus gambled his life and was close to death. Paul also anticipated that his life would be poured out like a drink offering (Philippians 2:17) and there is a moving passage where he describes how he cannot decide whether it is better to strike camp and be with Christ or to remain and help the church on earth (Philippians 1:20–25). God can be glorified both by our living and by our dying. Paul himself had been driven towards faith by the glory of God revealed in the dying of Stephen.

At one time, all missionaries were short-term missionaries. Most of them died in the first or second year of their service before they had even had the opportunity of learning the language well enough to preach the gospel properly. They would never have understood why today people *choose* to be only short-term missionaries when with improved medical aid we can live long enough not only to learn the language properly but also to spend a lifetime planting and perfecting churches overseas.

There is that question often asked at missionary meetings: Are you willing to go anywhere for Jesus Christ? If you have as good an imagination as I have, you can lose a lot of sleep over that question. Does the Lord want me to go and preach to the Eskimos and perhaps freeze to death in the Arctic? I heard of a missionary who dived into the Amazon river for a swim and all that came to the surface was his bathing trunks! If I went to Latin America I might be eaten alive by piranha, man-eating fish. Or does the Lord perhaps want me to go to India, where I might catch cholera and be dehydrated to death?

If you are imagining all the frightening situations you might meet or the horrible deaths you might die, I have a word of encouragement for you. You cannot possibly die in all these different ways – only in one of them! Let's get our foolish fears in proportion. God is not calling us to go anywhere but to some one particular where! Death is a possibility today wherever we live. My eldest boy was bitten by a venomous snake at home in England and my two oldest children have been shot at on different occasions by hooligans with air rifles in Britain.

At one time to become a missionary meant almost certain death and few ever expected to come home again. In the 17th and 18th centuries one in three Roman Catholic missionaries died on the voyage out either of disease or shipwreck. Today missionary deaths on the field are relatively uncommon and come to people as a great shock. The majority of missionaries live to a ripe old age.

The Lord Jesus asks us to take up the cross and deny ourselves because 'he gave himself for us'. I am sure that many of us would be prepared to die for him. Are we equally prepared to live for him? I want to ask you whether you are ready to give your *whole* life to serve Christ; to give the rest of your life, however long or short it is, for the Lord to use to build his church and extend his kingdom. Richard Baxter wrote:

If life be long I will be glad
That I may long obey;
If short, yet why should I be sad
To soar to endless day?

*Check: Are you willing to make sacrifices in each of these five areas?
What are they? Pray about each one in turn.*

Five
Is it worth it?

Objectives:
To demonstrate the great adventure and the privileges of cultural identification and to show that our lives are so enriched in Christ's service, that our anticipated sacrifices become blessings instead. God is not out to make us miserable, but to grant us immeasurable joy and fulfilment.

The previous chapter looked at only half of a biblical truth. It's true that if we try to save our lives we shall lose them. But now we go on to remind ourselves of the corresponding truth, that those who are ready to lose their lives for Jesus' sake will 'find' or 'save' them (Luke 9:24). This whole sacrifice idea can be terribly overdone. It only looks like sacrifice and loss beforehand when you cannot make up your mind whether to risk it or not. When you look back on it, you see that it was a gateway into the most wonderful life you could ask for.

Jesus' promise

Jesus expressed this very clearly. When Peter said, 'We have left everything to follow you', Jesus replied, 'I tell you the truth, no-one who has left home or brothers or sisters or mother or father or children or fields for me and the gospel will fail to receive a hundred times as much in this present age (homes, brothers, sisters, mothers, children and fields – and with them, persecutions) and in the age to come, eternal life' (Mark 10:28–30). This is true to experience. You have to 'leave' before you 'receive'.

As a student I wrestled with whether or not to consider missionary service, and made heavy weather of it with my foolish fears and exaggerated anticipations, but my life would have been immeasurably impoverished if I had not gone. Yes, it's true that the missionary lives on a relatively small income. But life is incredibly enriched in other ways. The missionary has friends of many nationalities all over the world – especially among those to whom he goes with the gospel. In my case it was Japanese friends. The ability to understand the Japanese language opened the door to the rich and varied ancient culture of Japan. With our children we climbed the country's volcanoes, swam from its beaches, ski'd on its mountain slopes and steamed ourselves in its hot springs. To get there our voyages by ship took us to Gibraltar, Naples, Egypt, Aden, Bombay, Colombo, Indonesia, Penang, Singapore and Hong Kong. From the ship we enjoyed watching flying fish and spouting whales. Later, our return route took us by sea across to Russia, by plane over Siberia to Moscow, then overland across Poland and Germany and so home again to England.

Children

When reading the previous chapter you may have thought that with all the parental absence they have to cope with, the children of the missionaries are a deprived lot. I remember my small son, aged three, making a sandcastle. When some condescending adult asked what it was, he replied: 'The Kremlin'.

'How funny: fancy a little boy like that making a model of the Kremlin. What does he know about it?'

'He's been there!' I said.

Possibly our children lacked what wealthy parents might have given. But in Japan they went skiing every lunchtime through the long winter at school, and later in Malaysia they enjoyed exotic holidays swimming over coral reefs, climbing streams in the jungle and chasing butterflies. They even went to school in the jungle, five thousand feet up in the mountains. They got used to intercontinental flights and they have friends all over the world. You could scarcely call them deprived: they have a wider view of the world than most adults in their own country.

I myself have enjoyed the astonishing privilege of visiting Christian communities in many parts of the world. I have spoken of the longhouses in Sarawak and the wonder of what the gospel has done. I remember sleeping in a three-walled hut among tribal Christians in Mindoro (Philippines) or eating freshly harvested rice with the Yao in North Thailand, and being invited to hear them sing 'I have decided to follow Jesus' in their own language. Or I think of another night in a Philippine village in Mindanao. None of the Christians had been believers longer than six months and the missionaries were only first-termers. After the day was over we went out for a short stroll and found a huge jungle tree lit up as with thousands of tiny hovering lights; I have never seen fireflies like it anywhere else. We caught a few in our hands, put them into a jar, and took them back to the simple hut the missionaries lived in. After we were all in our sleeping-bags in the darkness, we took the lid off the jar and watched the fireflies climb up into the roof, flicker and go out. We were laughing together like a bunch of kids.

You could scarcely call such missionary lives *dull*, could you?

I could never turn round to the Lord and complain that he blighted my life by calling me to his service. Sacrifice? Well, perhaps that's how some people think it was, and perhaps that is what I expected and was afraid of when I started – but now I can only thank God for making life so rich and varied.

Marriage

I feel rather sorry for married people who have not enjoyed the adventure of missionary life together, because it wonderfully strengthens and enriches a marriage. To think that, by refusing, one might have had a nine-to-five commuting life, coming home from some dull office to a captive housewife! There is real blessing in sharing adventures together, even the harder times: the slog of those five-month-long winters of ice and snow in northern Japan with nappies (diapers) hanging from the rafters day in, day out; when the toilet was at sixteen degrees of frost for six weeks on end and the eggs frozen solid and uncrackable. We can look back and remember those five-week-long ship journeys to and from Japan – seasick down below in the Bay of Biscay, ashore visiting the zoo in Colombo, on deck watching flying fish in the Indian Ocean. And when you are the only people of your own nationality for miles around, you are thrown into each other's company, and share things in a way many people miss. No two of our babies have ever been delivered by doctors of the same nationality, although they were born in only two countries (neither of them Britain) – but for toddlers we preferred the soft *tatami* matting of Japan to the hard stone floors of Singapore. We remember carrying babies on our backs up volcanoes, sliding them over the snow in a plastic kitchen bowl, and taking them on a boat in Thailand floods. When they were older they went off to Japanese kindergarten, caught squid off the coast of Malaysia, walked through mangrove swamps after mudskippers, and caught huge butterflies at saltlicks. As husband and wife we laughed at the richness of life with our growing family.

We shared in church-planting together – the heartbreak of a convert backsliding, the extraordinary privilege of baptizing new believers, tent evangelism at the cherry-blossom festival, the Japanese wedding receptions together in Tokyo and Singapore, not to mention Chinese weddings too. Missionaries in church-planting and evangelism are, I suppose, especially fortunate because husbands and wives can work together side by side in a way which is increasingly rare in these post-industrial revolution days. And this enriches their lives because each can love and respect the other as a Christian worker, as a colleague as well as a lover. Peter used to take his wife with him (1 Corinthians 9:5). Perhaps that's why he could come up with an expression like 'heirs with you of the gracious gift of life' (1 Peter 3:7).

And giving hospitality together to a multitude of missionary visitors; if not quite from every nation under heaven, it still feels like it. And sharing a hot bath together through the courtesy of a Japanese couple who knew there wasn't one in the missionaries' house.

We shared those evenings when the house was suddenly quiet after the teenage kids had left us at the airport, and my tears fell into the washing-up water when I played their favourite records. Or we have got into bed together feeling so forlorn after that airport farewell, only to find a note under the sheet:'Dear Mummy and Daddy, we know you find partings hard and so do we, but we want you to know that we wouldn't want to change our family life for anybody else's.'

The missionary life is good for marriage. You have to face the difficult and sad times together far away from your parents. A letter comes – your mother has died before you even knew she was ill. The sobs are there in your throat, but your wife's arms are there to comfort. And the riotous times – the hilarity of Christmas morning with small children opening parcels; the ecstasy of birth and the sadness of miscarriage. All these experiences, shared by any couple, somehow mean more when you are thousands of miles away from your country, and your partner is the only person to whom you can really express yourself properly without struggling in a difficult foreign language.

The apostle's experience

Paul is talking about his missionary work, when he tells the Romans 'I glory in Christ Jesus in my service to God' (15:17). William Barclay calls it ' a legitimate pride in my work'. I think I would say 'I revel in serving God.'

That's it. Paul *enjoys* his missionary service. He glories in his work, and he uses this word 'glorying' some fifty-eight times. There's a tremendous zest for life in the whole thing. Do you like your work? I love it, Paul exults. There is something so right, so fitting, so full of privilege and awe and wonder and bated breath about a whole life spent serving the Lord in such a way.

He has been talking about proclaiming the gospel (verse 16) and he says, 'It has always been my ambition to preach the gospel where Christ was not known' (verse 20). Far too many talks about missions and challenges to mission major on the sacrifice, the hardships and the difficulties. Paul talks about these as well, but it sticks out a mile that this man exults in the life his Lord has called him to. He wouldn't have had any other. This is the most rewarding life, to be a servant of Jesus Christ and a herald of his gospel.

Perhaps you know something of the joy of seeing one individual led to Christ. Then enlarge that a bit to imagine a whole family transformed. Then think of the privilege of being in at the start of a whole new congregation. I've been mainly in student work, and then in pastoral leadership, but even so there are two or three churches which I have had the privilege (together with others) of seeing the Lord bring into being. When Paul planted a church in Ephesus it remained there for 1400 years. There is not much that compares with this: writing books may be very satisfying when you hold in your hands a copy fresh from the press; but books go out of print remarkably quickly. And so many other things we do – talks we give, sermons we preach, minutes we take, letters we file, lectures we deliver – drain away into the sands of time very fast indeed. But a congregation of God's people is something else: it has life of its own from the Lord, and it goes on and on and grows down the years. I think you can look on planting churches as among the most satisfying kind of building there is: something lasting after we are dead and gone.

Think back to those converted headhunters in Sarawak – those Christian longhouses. Just think of the privilege of being the first missionary, and seeing what God has done in transforming the life of a whole community in this astonishing way. It might never have happened if three young Australians had not set out to work in the jungles of Borneo. And just think how they could have missed being in on that.

When I was a student there was no Christian work in Nepal at all. One of my contemporaries at university, after qualifying in medicine, was one of the first missionaries to go to Nepal, in the late fifties. Today there is a church of more than ten thousand believers, and it is still growing in spite of persecution and imprisonment. Just think of being able to say you had seen something like that happen in your lifetime – that you were in at the beginning of a work of God. In one sense there is no glory for us: Paul in the same passage says: 'I will not venture to speak of anything except what Christ has accomplished through me' (Romans 15:18). Often nothing does happen until we get desperate and really start to pray. There is always a sense too of being a humble spectator of what God is doing. It seems almost as if he acts in spite of us and our feeble faith and our inadequate efforts. And usually it's not a single individual but a team of different people together whom the Lord uses. But what a privilege to be a spectator: and how dreadful to think of missing something like that if this is where the Lord wants you to be. And there are still places left in the world where you could be one of the pioneers and see God work miracles in your brief lifetime. There are still a few missionaries left who entered Nepal in 1953 before there were any Christian churches in that country at all. The great Korean church is

74

not a hundred years old yet and there are a few old people whose lives span its history. It is a great privilege to be one of the first pioneers in a new area of missionary advance, as we move in and wait for the Lord to give the 'increase'.

Do you have that passionate desire to preach the gospel to people who have never heard of it before? 'Those who were not told about him will see, and those who have not heard will understand' says Paul quoting Isaiah. Livingstone was haunted by the smoke of a thousand African villages he saw in the distance. I remember climbing a Japanese volcano and looking over a green sea of rice before me. Among those paddy-fields were small brown islands – scores of farming villages where Christ had not been preached (and probably still has not in most of them, except by Christian radio programmes). To stand on the frontiers of Christendom, the growing edge of the kingdom and press on beyond the borders as a pioneer, knowing that if you had not gone it would be waiting still – that is what it means to be a missionary servant of a missionary Christ.

> We are the pilgrims, master; we shall go
>   Always a little further: it may be
> Beyond that last blue mountain barred with snow
>   Across that angry or that glimmering sea.

James Elroy Flecker from *Hassan*.

The garden of the Lord

The earth is the Lord's and the fullness thereof – and if you walk with him, he will show it to you like a man taking you round his garden. God is no man's debtor. He means what he says. 'He who loses his life for my sake *will find it.*'

When I was a student I was offered the opportunity of a free skiing trip to Switzerland. It was something I had never done and would have loved to do. The trouble was there was also a need for workers on a schools campaign in Birkenhead, across the Mersey from Liverpool. Birkenhead certainly didn't compare with Grindelwald. So should I grab what I might never get a chance to do again? It was a struggle, but in the end I went up to Merseyside to preach the gospel to those schoolboys. I thought I would never have another opportunity for such a marvellous skiing trip. But then God sent us to Japan, where for some years we lived within an hour of good ski slopes, and could take our children too. Sacrifice? He never does things by halves if you take him seriously.

To borrow the apostle's apology, excuse a little boasting! The Lord has taken me on his business to every continent except Latin America. I've caught salmon in New Zealand, watched birds in sight of Annapurna in the Himalayas, sailed in Australia, come down the rapids of the Mekong, ski'd in the Rockies, photographed alpine plants in the Swiss Alps, and seen the Victoria Falls where there is a superb statue of David Livingstone, the first white man to see them – and all that just on days off!

I have watched pelicans in South Australia and penguins in Victoria and albatross in New Zealand, a wallcreeper in Switzerland, snow geese in Vancouver and humming-birds in California. We grew orchids on the balcony of our flat in Singapore, alpine plants in England and beautiful spring shrubs in Japan. Missionaries have always revelled in God's creation: William Carey had a botanical garden, while the pioneers of the gospel in Nepal made their first surveys on bird-watching expeditions (and then got invited to stay).

Then there are the riches of exploring another culture: to wake up after a night spent on one's soft mattress spread on the matting with the morning sun streaming through the paper squares between the natural wood lattice of the sliding windows; the simplicity of the room with its focus on the alcove and its eye-catching flower arrangement and the hanging scroll – what a pleasure! Or the cheerfulness of the Chinese ten-course dinner eaten at leisure with good friends, the variety of tastes and the blessing of rice to the palate. Or the open friendliness of the Malay boatmen as they shoot the rapids in Pahang, or float soundlessly downriver in the late afternoon hearing every bird and tree-frog and the mysterious plop of some vanishing creature.

'How many are your works, O Lord! In wisdom you made them all; the earth is full of your creatures. There is the sea, vast and spacious, teeming with creatures beyond number – living things both large and small' (Psalm 104:24–25). And that could set me off again about the incredible variety of fishes to be seen when you swim around a coral reef . . . the Creator is so lavish. He will give you the desires of your heart, without measure, pressed down and running over. Yes, there is sacrifice; you must lose your life for him, in order to find it. But sacrifice is balanced with blessings.

All these things will be added to you

It's a basic Christian truth: seek first the kingdom of God and his righteousness and *all these things* will be added. It's true.

There is a spiritual blessing in having to rethink the gospel and your understanding of it, and express it in an entirely new set of words in another language. You must build a new apologetic to explain the unchanging spiritual truths of the Bible in terms of a fresh set of cultural presuppositions. In Japan you have to scrap the illustrations from cricket and drop-scones, and explain them now in terms of sumoo wrestling and *sashimi* (raw fish). You have to drop illustrations from Scrooge or Winnie-the-Pooh, and try the writings of Kikuchi Kan or *kabuki* (Japanese opera).

There is exhilarating blessing in being able to preach the saving gospel in a language different from your own, and, in spite of the lisping, stammering tongue, seeing the Holy Spirit working and people coming to Christ. And to have friends – lifelong friends whose culture is quite different from yours, and memories of them with you always, aided by slides and photographs! You even grow new roots in other countries and cultures. There is emotion and privilege in that too. You rather pity those who know the nationals of other countries only in terms of familiar distorted stereotypes and popular clichés.

It would be folly and stupidity to feel that we had made any significant sacrifices at all: or that our life had been anything but enriched as its horizons widened immeasurably.

And, best of all, God has been pleased to work mightily through our feeble efforts. We have been, in our puny human way, of some use to the Lord to whom we belong and whom we serve.

'He will find it . . .' this scripture *is* true.

You do not need to be afraid of God, or of what he will do if you put your life into his hands without reserve. He will not curse you or cramp your life into a narrow mould, but will abundantly bless you. He has promised to do so, and he is quite determined to bless you.

So why don't you let him?

Check: You have one life to live: so how and when will you use it?

PRAYER
Now put this book down, and tell your Lord what is in your heart about the way you want to spend your life for him.

Six
Am I called?

Objective:
To clarify the nature of the missionary call in order to remove that paralysis which results when people wait for some sensational experience that Scripture nowhere universally promises. And to help people make up their minds and take positive steps.

You might think from the enthusiasm of the previous chapter that every Christian ought to be a church-planting missionary. No. Not quite every Christian! It is a matter of guidance and the 'missionary call'. But what do we mean by the 'missionary call'? People often use the expression without defining carefully what is meant. This causes a great deal of confusion. Some individuals feel strongly drawn to a particular country or people, or to a particular kind of Christian work and therefore refer to having been 'called' to such work. Other people, convinced of the need to make disciples of all nations, and of the lost state of people without Christ, passively wait for some remarkable piece of supernatural guidance; and when it doesn't come they remain in a kind of spiritual limbo thinking they haven't been 'called'.

Some missionary societies even ask the candidate whether he feels 'called' to work with them. At first sight this seems to arise from an exaggerated sense of self-importance, but when pressed, most missionary societies will admit that all they are really asking is whether the individual feels happy with their particular ethos. Sometimes individuals quote a biblical verse as constituting in some special way their guidance. As we shall see, it is far from easy to substantiate all this from Scripture, or to show that the missionaries sent out in the Acts of the Apostles always had direct supernatural guidance for everything that they did.

What then does the Bible teach us about the 'missionary call'?

The general call to the whole church

Traditionally evangelical missions base a great deal upon the missionary commands of the Lord Jesus, particularly in the closing verses of Matthew's Gospel:

> Then Jesus came to them and said, 'All authority in heaven and on earth has been given to me. Therefore go and make disciples of all nations, baptizing them in the name of the Father and of the Son and of the Holy Spirit, and teaching them to obey everything I have commanded you. And surely I will be with you always, to the very end of the age.'

—with occasional side-glances at Luke 24:47:

> . . . and repentance and forgiveness of sins will be preached in his name to all nations, beginning at Jerusalem.

— and John 20:21:

> Again Jesus said, 'Peace be with you! As the Father has sent me, I am sending you.'

—while Acts 1:8 is also frequently referred to:

'. . . But you will receive power when the Holy Spirit comes on you; and you will be my witnesses in Jerusalem, and in all Judea and Samaria, and to the ends of the earth.'

There was a tendency on the part of the Protestant Reformers to regard these as no more than commands to the original apostles, but Justianus von Welz in Germany and later William Carey in England expounded the Great Commission in Matthew 28 as imperative for the church in every age. Manifestly the promise to be with us lasts 'always, even to the very end of the age', and it therefore seems reasonable to believe that the command is also of permanent relevance for the same period.

Moreover the command is clearly self-perpetuating. That is, the first apostles went in obedience to Christ, made disciples, baptized them and taught them everything Christ commanded. Since that teaching must have included this particular great command of Jesus, the first converts also made disciples, baptized them and taught them to obey all of Christ's commands including the final one, so that they in turn made more disciples, baptized them and commanded them, and so on.

These marching orders of the Christian church have never been rescinded. The church does not need to wait for any additional guidance before it goes out to make more disciples. Indeed according to words with a similar ring a few chapters earlier in Matthew, 'This gospel of the kingdom will be preached in the whole world as a testimony to all nations, and then the end will come' (24:14).

So this process which Jesus set in motion is to continue until the end comes. It is a command for every baptized disciple, who is bound to obey it if he owns Jesus as Lord. It means that the whole Christian church is committed to mission: the church is a world-wide evangelization society concerned to take the gospel to all nations. There is no suggestion of peaceful coexistence with other religious traditions, old or new. It is an uncompromising imperialism in service of the one described in Revelation 1:5 as 'the ruler of the kings of the earth'.

In this general sense, every committed Christian, as a disciple of Jesus, is called to mission. If God is a missionary God, then his church is a missionary church. Every Christian accepted a missionary call when he was baptized as a disciple. In this sense no one group of Christians is more missionary than any other; we have all been called to make disciples: it is a project to which the whole church is committed.

The role call

The New Testament is equally clear that all Christians are called to exercise some role or function in the local church. Every believer is expected to exercise one or more gifts from among a variety of gifts within the body of the local congregation. Though the whole church is called to mission, there is some division of labour and different functions are exercised by different members of the local body. Several passages emphasize the variety of roles to be exercised by different members (*e.g.* Romans 12:3–8; 1 Corinthians 12:4–27; Ephesians 4:7–16). Again, there are no first- or second-class Christians in regard to gifts: just as every Christian is called, so every Christian is equipped by the Holy Spirit with a view to performing particular roles or functions in the local church. This is also the place where those spiritual gifts are first recognized and developed.

Thus Barnabas had already shown such a gift for exhortation that the Jerusalem church sent him to Antioch, where together with Saul he exercised a teaching ministry in that city. Having been sent out by the church, they are then called apostles (Acts 14:4, 14). Silas was already leader and prophet in the Jerusalem church when Paul invited him to join him on the second missionary journey (Acts 15:22, 32).

Not every role in the local church fits everyone to be a

82

church-planting apostle or evangelist, but clearly some particularly do. It is not enough to offer professional skills for missionary service, unless one has spiritual gifts to be effective in the church overseas. But again the missionary call is not something which sets someone apart from or above his fellow Christians: it is only that the church sets him aside to fulfil a missionary role. This is one role among many possible roles which a Christian may fulfil: but every Christian is called to fulfil some role.

The geographical call

Every Christian has to be born somewhere, live somewhere and work somewhere. Every Christian should want to be where God wants him to be: right bang in the centre of the circle of his will. No place is more holy than any other. Overseas, as one geographer remarked, is only 'an accident of continental drift'. Some Christians are told to stay put (like the apostles in Acts 8:1). Some are driven out by circumstances beyond their control and witness as they go (like those driven out of Jerusalem by persecution, described in Acts 11:19–21), while yet others are sent out by their fellows to cross seas and frontiers (like Paul and Barnabas in Acts 13:1–2). But again no Christian is superior to any other. All alike need a conviction that they are where God wants them to be, whether they stay in the place where they were born, whether they are moved by other circumstances or whether they quite deliberately cross frontiers in order to take the good news to people who have never heard it.

A 'missionary call', then, combines these three different aspects of 'call' we have looked at. A missionary is a Christian called (like all others) to make disciples of all nations; he manifests spiritual gifts appropriate to cross-cultural evangelism and church-planting, and he has a geographical call which takes him across frontiers away from his native land and family home. But all three aspects equally apply to all other Christians: the missionary shares all three with every other Christian, though his particular gifts and location make him an *overseas* missionary.*

How God called people in Acts

But how exactly does this geographical call work out? We have only one life to live, and even if we had nine there are far more than nine needy countries in which those lives might be spent preaching Christ, saving souls, baptizing bodies and planting churches. There are so many possibilities. So how do we get from where we are at the moment to where God wants us to be?

1. *Direct supernatural intervention*
Talks about the missionary call often focus on two special occasions in the experience of Paul of Tarsus when God intervened directly in an unmistakable and overtly supernatural way to tell his servants where to go.

The Holy Spirit specifically told the praying leaders in Antioch to set aside Barnabas and Saul to the work for which he had called them (Acts 13:2). Later, when they were already missionaries, and working in Troas, Paul had a vision in the night of a certain man of Macedonia who appealed: 'Come over to Macedonia and help us' (Acts 16:9).

But this direct supernatural intervention is in Acts only one of the many ways that the Lord used to get his servants from one place to another. The second missionary journey actually began with a common-sense decision, and the third journey began in a straightforward way without any mention of specific guidance.

---

* It is possible to construct a fourth category of a special missionary call from Acts 26:16–18, Galatians 1:15–16, but it seems better to use the framework I have suggested in order to avoid any hierarchy of spirituality.

84

2. Sensible and responsible planning

The second journey was initiated when Paul said to Barnabas, 'Let us go back and visit the brothers in all the towns where we preached the word of the Lord and see how they are doing' (Acts 15:36). This was a responsible act: they had planted some small struggling churches, in the face of considerable opposition and persecution as well as false teaching. It was a responsible and sensible thing to go back there again to give them further teaching and encouragement.

After he left Ephesus, and revisited the churches in Macedonia and Achaia, Paul learned of a plot being formed against him when he was in Corinth. So 'he *decided* to go back through Macedonia' (20:3). Again this was a sensible thing to do. Another instance is in Romans 1:13 where Paul says 'I *planned* many times to come to you'. God can guide us in many ways. Sometimes he chooses to do it in a manifestly supernatural way, but at other times the Christian, indwelt by the Holy Spirit, prayerfully trusting the Lord to guide him, is able to plan using sanctified common sense, knowing that the Holy Spirit can guide him through this means too if he chooses.

3. Circumstantial guidance

Christian work was often initiated and the gospel often spread as a result of persecution. Thus the persecution that arose over Stephen scattered the Jerusalem church throughout Judea and Samaria, where Philip preached. Those who were scattered went everywhere preaching the word (Acts 8:1–4). Others, leaving Jerusalem for the same reason, went up the coast to Phoenicia, across to Cyprus and up to Antioch, where they started preaching to Greeks (11:19–20). It was persecution that sent Paul and Barnabas on from town to town, and later Paul and Silas out from Thessalonica, to Berea and then to Athens (17:10–15).

Before the second missionary journey there was a serious difference of opinion between Paul and Barnabas that led to their parting, but the result was that Barnabas and Mark went to Cyprus, and Paul took Silas through Galatia (15:39–40).

Today, too, circumstances such as war, political problems, persecutions and internal church difficulties can play a part in God's guidance and the spread of the gospel.

4. *Invitation by believers*

Paul was required to stay longer at Ephesus (Acts 18:19–20), but refused, saying 'I will come back if it is God's will', which he subsequently did (19:1). Peter responded positively to the urgent request from the disciples in Joppa when they came to Lydda following Tabitha's death (9:38). He would not have responded so positively to the invitation to go to Caesarea with the Gentile messengers of Cornelius, had it not been for the vision and the clear impulse from the Holy Spirit (Acts 10). But on the earlier occasion it was a straightforward response to a call from people in need.

We should take seriously calls for help from God's people. My own mission-call came as a direct invitation from Japanese student workers to join them in working among students in Japan.

5. *Sending by churches*

When the church in Jerusalem heard of the number of Greeks who had turned to the Lord in Antioch as a result of preaching by men of Cyprus and Cyrene, they 'sent Barnabas' off to Antioch (Acts 11:22). Nothing is said about supernatural guidance, or even Barnabas' own sense of call. There is just a matter-of-fact statement that the church saw a need and sent one of their number off to meet it. This involvement of the church in sending its members on evangelistic and missionary journeys is an important aspect of the missionary call.

Even very young churches acted responsibly in this way. When persecution arose in Thessalonica and then in Berea, 'the brothers' in both towns took action to send Paul away out of trouble (Acts 17:10, 14). Paul wisely seems to have accepted their guidance, although they were relatively young in the faith.

6. *Responsibility to return to the sending church*
The apostles needed no supernatural guidance to return home to the church which had commissioned them and sent them out in the first place. It was a responsible thing to return to them and report back on what the Lord had done. The first return (Acts 14:26) speaks of this 'furlough' spent with the home church, and following their visit to the council of Jerusalem, it was further prolonged (15:35). The same thing was repeated after the second missionary journey (18:22–23).

This was no less under the guidance of the Lord than the initial sending out. The Lord is as able to guide by normal common-sense means as by supernatural means. We go wrong when we insist that he must guide using any one particular method: the choice is always his as sovereign Lord of the harvest.

7. *Chosen by missionary leaders*
It is instructive to notice that sometimes a person's involvement in Christian work could result from an invitation from a Christian leader to join him in the work in which he was already involved. This closely parallels the situation of missionary groups in the present-day situation. Thus when Barnabas was sent to Antioch he first went to Tarsus to enlist Paul's aid in the teaching ministry in the new Antioch congregation (Acts 11:25). Later Paul chose Silas (15:40) and then Timothy (16:3) to accompany him on his missionary invasion of Europe. It is clear that this was based on Paul's knowledge of the spiritual gifts and qualities of the individuals chosen.

8. *Sent by missionary leaders*
There is often discussion as to how far modern missionary

87

societies find any equivalent in the New Testament. It certainly seems that the missionary band with Paul as its leader made its own decisions, apart from either the church which sent them out (communications made that impossible) or the church that they were currently seeking to bring into being.

While in Ephesus, Paul '*sent* two of his helpers, Timothy and Erastus, to Macedonia' (Acts 19:22). Writing to the Thessalonians from Corinth, Paul explains how he *sent* Timothy to Thessalonica to encourage them and to bring back news of them to the anxious apostle (1 Thessalonians 3:2). On other occasions he *sent* Tychicus (Colossians 4:8) and to Philippi he anticipated *sending* Timothy and did *send* Epaphroditus (Philippians 2:19, 23, 25).

In other words, another way the Lord guides is through the leadership of others in a team of Christian workers. Guidance does not need to be personal and individual. It may come through other responsible Christians.

Guidance

This brief study of guidance in the Acts shows that God is not limited to any one form of guidance. He has different ways of guiding people to move to one place or away from another. Therefore the individual looking for geographical guidance or a clear missionary call should not expect the Lord to call him in one particular way.

The individual who is ready and willing to go anywhere the Lord may direct, and who has a concern to preach Christ to those who have never heard and to plant new churches in places where they do not yet exist, may be guided through any or all of these different means: through the church to which he belongs, through the invitation of others, through Christian leaders, through circumstances, through common-sense recognition of responsibility, through sensible planning and many other ways. There may or may not be more obviously supernatural guidance as well. We should not delay or dither because we have not yet seen a vision of a Macedonian or an angel. These are possible means of guidance, but, as we have seen, not the only ones. The more 'mundane' forms of guidance are no less divine guidance than any other.

Response to the missionary call

Outlining the principles is helpful, but all of us as individuals still have to work our way through a number of decisions and stages of preparation for service. I want to explain these one by one and then summarize them as a final check-list.

1. *Willingness*
There are people who get worried and fearful lest the Lord might call them to overseas service. Some young men and women contemplating engagement and marriage may fear that their intended partner might want to drag them off to the ends of the earth. Some people are just not willing to go. Others tend to add conditions – 'As long as I don't have to go to a hot country'; or 'as long as I don't have to go somewhere very primitive.' A basic condition, then, is a willingness to go anywhere and to do anything that the Lord may direct, recognizing that his will and purpose are good and wonderful and not something to be afraid of.

It is often at this point that the greatest struggle takes place. Although we are in some sense committed to the Lord Jesus, we are reluctant to recognize his right to send us anywhere. The problem resolves itself when we realize that acknowledging Jesus as Lord means being willing to accept his direction for my life.

Where he sends, I will go; where he leads, I will follow; what he commands, I will do.

2. *Availability*
Often the people most willing to go are the ones least able to

respond. Physical and emotional health are normal pre-requisites for most cross-cultural missionary work. Disabilities like diabetes or asthma, or a past history of depression or other nervous illness, almost certainly make it unwise to expose the person to new pressures. Pioneer tribal work requires a strong pair of legs. I am always impressed by the way in which people with serious disabilities are often so willing and eager, when fully healthy individuals are sometimes not.

Family responsibilities are another consideration. If you are already married with three or four children, then that raises serious questions as to the advisability of disrupting the whole family, quite apart from the great expense involved. It is very hard for a mother with toddlers to learn a foreign language. Young people considering missionary service do well to delay marriage, and certainly to delay starting a family until the wife has had a chance to learn the language. An individual may also be responsible for a dependent parent, where there are no other brothers or sisters. It is a proper biblical responsibility to care for one's relatives (1 Timothy 5:8). Any of these factors may make a Christian unavailable or unsuitable for missionary work.

3. *Spiritual gifts*
As we have seen, suitability for service in a wider sphere is determined by the extent to which the would-be missionary has developed a role and exercised a ministry. The local church, and to a certain degree para-church Christian groups, give opportunity to develop and cultivate spiritual gifts in teaching, evangelism and leadership. The question, 'In what ways do you think you have something to contribute to the church overseas?' can be answered only by reference to gifts already manifested and usefulness already demonstrated in one's home church. The missionary of tomorrow is active and involved in his own home church today.

This may mean delay. We may be willing and available

90

but so far lacking in experience of Christian service. The missionary society may properly say, 'You must first give proof of missionary potential by a further period of training in your local church'. Well-developed churches such as those in Indonesia or Korea may even wish you to have full-time pastoral experience in your own country before going to them at all. In other cases, for pioneer work, a mission may advise you to spend a period working under your own minister or in another suitable congregation in order to enlarge your practical experience.

4. *Corporate confirmation*

We have seen already how large a part fellow Christians and the local church may play in guidance. However independent you are (a good quality in missionaries) you must not be individualistic (a bad quality). You should therefore seek the guidance of Christian leaders in your own local church, and other Christian friends, to see whether or not they are able to give some objective confirmation to your subjective sense of call. If they agree that they themselves long thought that you had demonstrated such qualities that would make you a suitable missionary candidate, that confirms it. If they are very doubtful, and point out glaring defects in your Christian character, or deficiencies in your Christian service, then you are manifestly not yet suitably prepared or qualified.

Training is often an expensive matter; and the willingness of your home church to contribute towards Bible and theological training is often an index of the extent to which they believe you are indeed called and are prepared to stand behind you as a church. If they are prepared to support you financially, it shows that they do indeed recognize in you the necessary abilities and skills. If they are not, then you need to discover exactly why.

5. *Training*

In missionary work it is commonly necessary to learn at

least one foreign language, sometimes more. Because we are so used to our English Bibles (only a translation, not the original!) we shall have considerable problems in rethinking the gospel in terms of an entirely different language using a different translation. A period of full-time training in order to grasp more clearly the teaching of the whole of Scripture, the original background against which it was written and the ways in which to tackle a new cultural situation, is regarded as a necessity by all responsible missionary societies. National Christian workers overseas will have had training, and will not respect you if you are manifestly ignorant. 'What does this person have to teach us?' some Japanese asked concerning one new missionary recruit.

That training must not be merely academic or theoretical. It must also include instruction about the world views of other religions, how to learn a language and how to understand and identify with a different culture, as well as training in all aspects of Christian service. We shall need teaching in pastoral theology, church growth and evangelism. We shall need experience of visiting, open-air preaching, pastoral care and many other practical matters. All this needs to be taken seriously, and most people will need to spend at least two years at it. An ambassador for Christ needs no less training than those in any other calling.

6. *Geographical location*

At first sight this seems a vast problem because there are so many possibilities. How can you determine which of them is the most needy and the one to which you are most suited?

In fact it is less complex than it appears, because factors like church tradition, language aptitude, practical skills and experience may in fact limit the places in which you could serve. Countries like Korea and Indonesia are principally Presbyterian in church order (Lutheran in Sumatra) and there are fewer openings for Baptists. The reverse is true in countries like Japan, Thailand and the Philippines where there are probably more opportunities for Baptists because the national churches in those countries now are principally in that tradition. Again Korean, Japanese and Chinese dialects demand a higher degree of aptitude than Indonesian, Philippine or Borneo languages. Some countries, such as Nepal, may require a professional qualification in medicine, agriculture or education in order to gain admittance.

All of this means that long-term exposure to information from a wide spectrum of countries is important even if you begin to narrow your interest down to a smaller group of countries or types of work. When I was a student we used to have a slogan: 'Something about everywhere, and everything about somewhere', indicating that we need both a wide general knowledge of God's work around the world, and detailed, specific knowledge of some particular area as a focus for interest and prayer. Joining various missionary groups is one of the best ways to gain this kind of information. If your church or Christian Union does not already include these in its programme, you could start one yourself by arrangement with the appropriate leaders. Missionary societies will be able to tell you whether there is a prayer group for their workers in your locality. If you go to Bible College you will find several groups, focusing on different areas of the world. The book *Operation World* by Patrick Johnstone (STL) or the small prayer cards for needy countries published by Operation Mobilisation are also very helpful ways of gaining a wide knowledge of facts and figures and a grasp of church situations in various lands.

The decision
Looked at in one way, each of us is a bit like a computer into which various data and experiences are fed till the answer eventually comes out. Looked at in another way, we are servants of God and can be certain that if we prayerfully seek his guidance he will indeed direct our lives. These two processes are not mutually contradictory, for God in his sovereignty will sift the information we obtain, and guide

the way we react, in such a way as to lead us through our normal thought-processes.

The *relative need* in different countries will be significant: countries with many Christians and many churches manifestly do not need international reinforcement to the same extent as small struggling groups of Christians in countries or districts where there are few or hardly any Christian churches at all.

Linguistic ability may be a negative indicator. If you are of only moderate ability then you would be wiser to avoid the more difficult languages. It is possible to take a Modern Language Aptitude Test which, while not absolute, is still a useful guide. Your results may rule out certain countries and point to others where the language requirements are less demanding. But the difficulty of language is often exaggerated. Most people who want to communicate in a new environment where they must either learn to understand and speak or remain silent, do steadily develop a facility in the new language.

We have already touched on *compatibility with the missionary society*, but I would like to say a little more about this important factor. It seems sensible to investigate a number of societies working in the area in which you are interested. It is often helpful to talk to field missionaries about their experience of what actually happens 'on the ground'. What it says in the society's literature and what actually happens are not always the same thing. Printed brochures are nearly always more idealistic than realistic, and it is as well to know this from the start. If you can get a national Christian's view of the missionary societies working in the area, that helps too. When I discovered that one missionary society in Africa never allowed Africans farther into their homes than the veranda (this was twenty-five years ago), I dropped that society from any further consideration.

But even more important is a sense of compatibility with the society's workers themselves. Every group has its own ethos: some very intense, others truly spiritual; some have their own treasured distinctiveness which does not always strike chords with us. So get in among them, go to their conferences and prayer meetings and sense the vibes. Make sure that you resonate with them! It's no good going out with a mission if you are full of reservations and misgivings about them as a group. It is important that you respect their leaders, appreciate your fellow missionaries and are thoroughly committed to their goals. They will want that too. After all, you could be with them for the rest of your life, and one day you might be asked to accept leadership responsibility within the organization. So it is important that you can identify fully with them.

Bearing all of these things in mind you will have to make a number of decisions. You will have to talk with the leaders of your church to decide about your call; decide where to get Bible and theological training, decide about marriage and when to start a family, decide about countries and decide about a missionary society. But remember that the Lord of the harvest and the Head of the church is even more concerned about where you serve him than you are. So there is no need to get all anxious and uptight about this decision-making process. You can relax, because you can trust him to guide you, over-rule your mistakes and put you into those places where your life will be most fruitful and most useful for his greatest glory.

'Do not be anxious about anything, but in everything, by prayer and petition, with thanksgiving, present your requests to God' (Philippians 4:6).

Check list:
1. Am I willing? To go anywhere? To do anything?
2. Am I available? Healthy? Without responsibilities?
3. Am I equipped – active and gifted in Christian service already?
4. Is my call confirmed by my home church? By Christian friends?
5. Am I trained? Theologically? Pastorally?

6. Am I clear about where the Lord wants me to go? Have I sufficient information? Have I been praying about a particular place?
7. Do I see a clear need for workers in a particular place?
   Do I have the necessary language aptitude for that place?
   Do I fit denominationally with the church there?
   Do I feel at one with the missionary group?
   Do I know the confirming witness of the Holy Spirit in my heart?